Human Rights as a Western Concept

Human Rights
As a Western Concept

Raimundo Panikkar
Arvind Sharma

D.K. Printworld (P) Ltd.
New Delhi

Cataloging in Publication Data — DK
[Courtesy: D.K. Agencies (P) Ltd. <docinfo@dkagencies.com>]

Panikkar, Raimon, 1918-
Human rights as a western concept / Raimundo Panikkar, Arvind Sharma.
vii, 103 p. 23 cm.
Includes bibliographical references (p.)
ISBN 8124604290

1. Human rights. I. Sharma, Arvind, joint author. II. Tittle.

DDC 323 22

ISBN 81-246-0429-0
First published in India in 2007

Published and printed by:
D.K. Printworld (P) Ltd.
Regd. Office: 'Sri Kunj', F-52, Bali Nagar
Ramesh Nagar Metro Station
New Delhi-110 015
Phones: (011) 2545-3975; 2546-6019; *Fax*: (011) 2546-5926
E-mail: dkprintworld@vsnl.net
Website: www.dkprintworld.com

Preface

THE question of the universality of human rights has two major dimensions to it. These are the theoretical and the political. The theoretical dimension was the first to emerge and was already an issue, when the Universal Declaration of Human Rights was in the process of being drafted.[1] It has also remained an issue since then right down to this day, not only in relation to the Declaration in general but also in relation to its particular provisions.[2]

The political dimension took more time to emerge but was clearly discernible at the U.N. World Conference on Human Rights at Vienna in 1993. As Charles Norchi observed: "For the first time since the Universal Declaration was adopted in 1948, countries not thoroughly steeped in the Judeo-Christian and natural law traditions are in the first rank. That unprecedented situation will define the new international politics of human rights. It will also multiply the

---

1. See Mary Ann Glendon, *A World Made New: Eleanor Roosevelt and the Universal Declaration of Human Rights*, (New York: Random House, 2001) *passim*.
2. See Tore Lindholm, W. Cole Durham, Jr. and Bahia G. Tahzib-Lie, eds., *Facilitating Freedom of Religion or Belief: A Deskbook* (Leiden, The Netherlands: Koninklijke Brill NV, 2004) pp. xxviii-xxxi, 76, pp. 351-52.

occasions for conflict."[3] It was not long before this prediction was fulfilled in a rather dramatic manner. The then Prime Minister of Malaysia Mohammad Mahathir proclaimed in 1996 that "Asian values are universal values. European values are European values."[4] The confrontation could not be more stark.

It is the political dimension which highlights the seriousness of the issue but the resolution of the issue is more likely to be promoted by a detailed and evenhanded discussion of the theoretical dimension of the issue. This book is designed to promote such a discussion.

---

3. As cited in Samuel P. Huntington, *The Clash of Civilizations and the Remaking of the World Order*, (New York: Simon & Schuster, 1996) pp. 196-97.
4. Cited, ibid., p. 109.

Contents

1

Introduction

THE famous declaration of human rights, adopted by the United Nations on 10 December 1948, is known as the Universal Declaration of Human Rights. The putative universality of human rights, however, became an issue as soon as it was adopted and has remained one ever since.

This book which you are about to read is one attempt to engage this multifaceted issue. It consists of two contributions. The first one is by Professor Raimundo (now Raimon) Panikkar. The second piece is a response to it by Arvind Sharma. The contribution of Professor R. Panikkar originally appeared as an article in the journal *Diogenes*, in the winter of 1982. A response to it was prepared by Arvind Sharma and shared with Professor Panikkar. Both agreed that this exchange might further the discussion of the vexed issue of the universality of human rights. Hence this book.

II

The rest of this Introduction offers some general remarks on the issue of the universality of human rights, as a way of leading into the exchange.

One may like to begin by recognizing that, in an earlier stage of its formulation by the Third Committee,[1] the

1. See Mary Ann Glendon, *The World Made New: Eleanor Roosevelt and the Universal Declaration of Human Rights*, New York: Random House, 2001, pp. 136-37.

declaration had been slated as an International Declaration of Human Rights.[2] Mary Ann Glendon notes:

> As soon as the committee wound up its review of the draft declaration, a subcommittee on style chaired by Cassin began to put everything into final form. At this stage a few changes were made in the sequence of articles, and the title was officially changed from "International Declaration of Human Rights" to the "Universal Declaration of Human Rights". The new title had been in casual use for some time, but Cassin, who proposed the official change, rightly considered the name to be of utmost significance. The title "Universal", he later wrote, meant that the declaration was morally binding on everyone, and not only on the governments that voted for its adoption. The universal declaration, in other words, was not an "international" or "intergovernmental" document; it was addressed to all humanity and founded on a unified conception of the human being.[3]

Thus, the naming of the declaration as a **universal** rather than an **international** document was not a mere lexical accident but marked a conceptual shift. It was of course possible to use the word **international** in this context, but the word **universal** included and also transcended it. That the two could be used virtually interchangeably at times is attested to by the fact that, when Charles Malik introduced the Universal Declaration on 9 December, 1948 he could still state that the declaration rested on a "firm international basis wherein no regional philosophy or way of life was permitted to prevail."[4]

---

2. Ibid., Appendix 5, p. 294.
3. Ibid., p. 161.
4. Cited, ibid., p. 165, emphasis supplied.

There is no denying the fact, however, that the description of the document as "universal" imparted to it a new kind of a dynamic, which could not be matched by the word international. One could, for instance, readily concede that the document was an international document, and yet debate its universality.

III

The concept of universality has been analyzed in several contexts by diverse scholars. Some of these discussions may be surveyed to determine if each involves an individual issue, or whether some or all issues point to the same or a similar problematic but in different ways.

1. Sometimes the word **universal** is contrasted with the word **global**. Ashis Nandy writes for instance that

> . . . globalization presumes that it is universal. Whereas it is only global, not universal. By universalism I mean that which has the capacity to transcend cultural, political and social systems. I don't think this globalization has that capacity. It tries to be universal by excluding a sizeable section of the world by either forgetting them or by declaring them irrelevant or superfluous. It has its own idea of universalism, picked up lock, stock and barrel from the post-war culture of the United States. But many of the cultures it is trying to displace, marginalize, or corner also have their own ideas of universalism. These versions clash.[5]

The implication of the application of the word universal, in the discourse on human rights in the present context,

---

5. *Talking India: Ashis Nandy in Conversation with Ramin Jahanbegloo*, New Delhi: Oxford University Press, 2006, p. 125.

may also be elaborated with the help of the following remarks by Upendra Baxi:

> The hegemony may globalize human rights without universalizing them. Globalization of human rights consists in those practices of governance by the dominant States that selectively target the enforcement of certain sets of rights or sets of interpretation of rights upon the "subaltern" State members of the world system. Such practices need no ethic of "universality" of human rights; these constitute an amoral exercise of dominant hegemonic power because the hegemony does not accept as a universal norm that its sovereign sphere, rife with human (*sic*) and human rights violations, ought to be equally liable to similarly based intrusions.[6]

He goes on to say:

> These summary observations commend the distinction I make between two orders of discursivity: **globalization** and the **universality of human rights**. Globalization of human rights necessarily fragments their vaunted universality, which makes problematic practices of production of the politics of human rights. The discourse concerning "relativism" remains deeply diversionary when this distinction gets overlooked in the theoretical and activist critique about the "universality" of human rights.[7]

Moreover:

> The practice of protection and promotion of universal human rights entails the construction of moral or ethical hierarchies of suffering. Such a construction takes place when certain rights (such as civil and political rights)

---

6. Upendra Baxi, *The Future of Human Rights*, New Delhi: Oxford University Press, 2002, pp. 95-96.
7. Ibid., pp. 96-97.

> stand prioritized over other human rights (such as social, economic and cultural rights). It occurs when even the former set of rights are subjected to the reason of the State, as when their suspension stands legitimated in "time of public emergency in the life of the nation." It occurs when solemn treaties prohibiting genocide and torture, cruel and degrading treatment or punishment, allow scope for reservations and derogations that eat out the very heart of remedies otherwise declared available for the violated.
>
> Not merely does the community of States construct such transactional hierarchies, but even human rights praxis *does so*. This makes human rights praxis at best *global* but not *universal*, with deep implications for the future of human rights.[8]

2. The term **universalism** is at times paired not with "globalism" but **relativism**. This happens, for instance, in the following extract:

> A more interesting way of looking at cultures is to see them as representing competing forms of universalism, not relativism. You are not saying that there is one culture that is at the pinnacle of human civilization and its artefacts and knowledge systems are universal, and all other cultures are legitimately different but must be understood in the language of the universal culture.

This may seem very unfair to cultural relativists, who technically include all cultures within the frame of cultural relativism. We are talking here of the shape the ideology has taken in popular culture. In that popular version, all cultures are equal under the banner of cultural relativism, but one of them has presumably accidentally produced the only universal ideas of development, nation-state, progress and modern science. Almost naturally, the

---

8. Ibid., pp. 117-18.

argument proceeds, that culture enjoys a clear priority in everything global, universal, cosmopolitan, or international. Modern scientific rationality is universal, so are human rights, concepts of good governance as practised in modern nation-states, secularism, history and development. There is a whole range of concepts that have been declared universal and protected from external criticisms and cultural contamination. You can criticize them from inside. You can talk of alternative or sustainable development, never of alternatives to development. You can talk of alternative history, never of alternatives to history. And these universals are seen as the specialization of one culture.[9]

3. Sometimes different conceptions of **universality** emerge in the context of the discussion of the **universality of science**, as in the following passage:

> Most people think that science cuts across cultures whereas values divide cultures. I sometimes suspect that basic human values cross cultural barriers more easily than do impersonal, cognitive orders, such as modern science. Values like non-violence, or better still, sanctity of life; the importance of a family or a community, any community; the protection of children, particularly infants, and a recognition of their vulnerability; the search for a sense of belongingness — these are always present in some incarnation in all societies. The dialogue between Gandhi and Andrews was not so much a common search for truth but a recognition that basic human values are shared and their various versions can be brought together or made to converse. The political trigger might have been Gandhi's insight, that Andrews had been marginalized in the British-Indian system, and that a culture that

9. *Talking India*, op. cit., pp. 141-42.

> marginalizes someone like Andrews could not have been in the best of health. Gandhi was probably pushed to establish an alliance with that part of English culture which Andrews represented, guessing that Andrews was fighting the same battle within his culture that he as an Indian was fighting with his.

Don't forget that Gandhi's voice too was for a long time the voice of a minority. The kind of militant non-violence he was talking about, the *satyagraha* he forged as a technique, the critique of modernity he offered, didn't enjoy absolute legitimacy in Indian culture — certainly not in the high culture of modern India. We don't have to believe the conventional wisdom of many people who come to India in search of gurus and spiritual bliss that this is a non-violent culture. There are a lot of restraints on violence in this culture — many injunctions, starting from the Jain and Buddhist scriptures to the Vaiṣṇava celebration of amity, but these injunctions do not make this a peaceful society. So, Gandhi was fighting a battle within Indian culture, and, for that battle, although he was in the minority in modern India and among the India elite, he could politically mobilize the masses for his cause. But that's a different story. Gandhi could see, he could appreciate the nature of the dissent that C.F. Andrews represented within Britain's ruling culture, and that was the strength of their dialogue. It was self-actualizing because it brought two recessive elements in two civilizations together. These elements were not powerful enough by themselves, but in coalition they became formidable.[10]

---

10. Ibid., pp. 147-48.

4. Sometimes **universalism** is contrasted with **parochialism**. Thus the Jewish author, Ruth Weiss, observes:

> Jewish "parochialism" is always implicitly universal, while Jewish law recognized both the legitimate existence of other peoples and the right of everyone who genuinely desired it to be a Jew. By contrast, universalist idealism in religion and politics is always repressive since it expects everyone to become its particular species of universalist.[11]

The same sentiment is also reflected in similar statements such as the following, that "universalism seeks to expand its borders, while particularity merely patrols them."

5. Sometimes a distinction is drawn between **uniformity** and **unity**, as representing two forms of **universality**. If all the religions of the world adopted the *same* set of scriptures, it could be called a universal scripture. It is also true, however, that all the religions of the world, as they exist, tend to have a scripture, although it is not the same scripture. Having a scripture could thus be viewed as a universal phenomenon. All the religions can thus be united in having a scripture, without it having to be the same or universal scripture.

6. The **universality** of human rights may be apposed to the concept of a *just international order* in the following manner:

> "Contemporary" human rights discursivity addresses, however, the problematic of a *just international order*, that is, a world order based on promotion and protection of "human rights" *within* and *across* human societies, traditions and cultures. Respect for "human rights" or the right to be and remain human, entails a complex,

---

11. Ruth R. Weiss, *If I Am Not For Myself: The Liberal Betrayal of the Jews*, New York: The Free Press, 1992, p. 179.

interlocking network of meanings that have to be sustained, renovated and replenished, at *all* levels: individuals, associations, markets, States, regional organizations of the States and international agencies and organizations which constitute a new totality that now stands addressed by the logics and paralogics of human rights. This difference raises its own distinctive problems when we address the issue of "universality."[12]

7. The concept of universality may be placed in a Hegalian context "when he [Hegel] distinguishes between three "moments": **abstract universality, abstract particularity** and **concrete universality**. The first moment stands for "undifferentiated unity," the second for "the differentiation of identity and difference," and the third for "concrete universality," which is the full realization of individuality."[13]

8. Another word **universality** could be paired with is **minority**. In such a context:

   "Multiculturalism" conceived through the prism of polyethnic rights is, at the end of the day, an adaptation by liberal cultural traditions of universal human rights and standards. Such adaptations flourish outside Euro-American cultures too. In each the abstract universality and abstract particularity of human rights remain in tension with the concrete universality. What remains important is the fact that the universal human rights culture makes problematic the project of concrete universality. National definitions of minority rights become contested fields from the standpoint of the abstract universal and the abstract particular.[14]

---

12. Upendra Baxi, op. cit., p. 92.
13. Ibid., p. 93.
14. Ibid., p. 109.

9. Sometimes a distinction is drawn between the **universality** of human rights and their **universalizability**. Here the crux of the matter is that human rights are not merely universal but universalizable — or should be. Hence the following stirring call of Dr Abdullahi An-Na'im:

> Human rights advocates do not have a choice regarding religious discourse. Religious discourse is a reality for the vast majority of our constituencies, and if we do not take a stand on religious grounds in favour of human rights, that stand will be taken against human rights on the ground with which our own constituencies resonate the most. If you ask a Muslim to make a choice between Islam and human rights, I think the obvious answer will be, "I will stand by Islam." It's *only* when we can make Islam and human rights synonymous, in the thinking and feeling and motivation and action of our constituencies, that you can have a human rights world culture — globally, a human rights culture.
>
> But if we maintain the tension, if we reject the dialogue between religion and human rights as attempting to bridge two irreconcilable world views, then I think it is our cause, the cause of human rights, that is likely to lose. For this reason, I plead that the choices, for those who are secularly inclined and for those who are religiously inclined, be made in the common cause of human rights. And I plead that foreign policy choices, regarding Algeria or regarding Sudan or regarding Rwanda, will be choices of principle and not choices of expediency.[15]

---

15. John Kelsay and Sumner B. Twiss, *Religion and Human Rights*, New York: The Project for Religion and Human Rights, 1994, pp. 89-90.

10. **Universality** may be juxtaposed with **antifoundationalism**.

Scholars such as Alan Gewirth (in the *Community of Rights*, 1996) have argued for what may be called objective foundations for human rights. As against this:

> Antifoundationalists deny the need, and question the desirability, of moral reason furnishing universal bases for human rights. It is maintained by many, and in various ways, that there is no "historical power which makes for righteousness — a power called truth, or rationality," nor indeed are there forces that may bring the powerful, unjust and brutal people amidst us to a sense of universal human vengeful rights, "if not a vengeful superego, or, at the very least the offended majesty of Kant's tribunal of pure practical reason. . . ." It is also argued that universal human rights are simply impossible because what counts as "human" and as rights belonging to humans, are [*sic*] context-bound and tradition-dependent. There is no transcultural fact or being that may be called "human" to which universal human rights may be attached. Eduardo Rabossi (an Argentine jurist) has recently urged that the "human rights phenomenon has rendered human rights foundationalism outmoded and irrelevant."[16]

For Eduardo Rabossi, there has been an "enunciative explosion of human rights"[17] and "for him that fact is all that matters."[18]

11. Sometimes the concept of the **universal** is placed alongside that of the **absolute**. Melville Herskovits distinguishes

---

16. Upendra Baxi, op. cit., p. 97.
17. Ibid.
18. Ibid., pp. 97-98.

between the two as follows:

> *Absolutes* are fixed and, as far as convention is concerned, are not admitted to the variation, to differ from culture to culture, from epoch to epoch. *Universals*, on the other hand, are those least common denominators to be extracted from the range of phenomena the natural or cultural world manifests.[19]

This leads Upendra Baxi into drawing a useful distinction:

> "Modern" human rights logics were *absolutist*, not *universal*. "Contemporary" human rights are, in contrast, *universal* precisely because they deny the absoluteness of *any* positing of rights, although some human rights are said to be *near absolute*, as is the case with a handful of, and often contested, *jus cogens*. Also, the logic of universality is constantly bedevilled by "utilitarianism of rights," that is, by arguments from consequences. The universality of human rights symbolizes the *universality of the collective human aspiration to make power increasingly accountable, governance progressively just, and the state incrementally more ethical*. I know of no "relativist" strand of thought that contests this desideratum.[20]

12. Sometimes the word **universal** is contrasted with the word **Western**. This argument can work in a double-edged way. On the one hand, it could be claimed that the discourse of so-called human rights is Western and therefore need not apply to other parts of the world. This amounts to a forensic use of the distinction *against* the West. The West can, however, also deploy it forensically against the rest of the world by claiming that *only* the West possesses the (lofty) concept of human rights.

---

19. Cited, ibid., p. 105.

20. Ibid., Italics in the original.

Upendra Baxi faults both the approaches. He counters the first position by pointing out: "What is of interest here is the fact that the practices of politics *of* human rights converge here with those of the politics *for* human rights. The very regimes and cliques that deny freedom and dignity, canons of political accountability, and denounce human rights "universality" as a sinister imperial conspiracy find support from intellectual and social activists critiquing the "universality" in the same prose."[21]

He also counters the second position by noting:

> Free-floating historians of ideas keep telling us that Asian, African, or other "non-Western" traditions had no analogue to the expression "human rights", but neither had the "Western traditions" even the phrase "rights" till the "mid-nineteenth century". Indeed, the invention of the phrase "human rights" is very recent. Apart from the sociolinguistic discovery of novelty, nothing much follows! Undoubtedly, words and phrases carry burdens of histories, but histories also give rise to regimes of phrases that mould the future. Surely, the discourse on human struggles and movements that empower human beings in time, place and circumstance to resist oppression (whether in East Timor or Myanmar) is also entitled to the same order of privilege that historians of ideas or cultural anthropologists claim for themselves![22]

The distinction may also involve the realization that

> . . . the US, like all major powers — and this is true of all others like China and India as well — is an insular society. It spends most of the time looking inside. Most people, when they see CNN International, think they are watching

---

21. Ibid., p. 103.
22. Ibid., p. 104.

> what Americans are watching. Frankly, CNN International is never shown in America.[23]

It may also involve having to confront such arguments as the following:

> Look at the rule that says the head of the IMF (International Monetary Fund) must be a European and the head of the World Bank must be an American. And note that 3.5 billion Asians do not qualify for running either of the organizations at a time when the fastest-growing economies are in Asia.
>
> Clearly, you need to make major changes in the global order, but to make those changes the West has to make some sacrifices and it is very difficult for them to do that. They would rather maintain their positions of domination as long as possible. The reason I emphasize that is they only see the problem as being there, not here. What I am telling them is that while the West is often part of the solution, it is also part of the problem. They have to see how they are contributing to the problem.[24]

This pairing of Western and universal is pervasive. John Gray writes for instance, in a review of the book: *The Writing on the Wall: China and the West in the 21st Century* by Will Hutton, as follows:

> A decade ago policy-makers and opinion-formers were supremely confident that globalization meant the spread of Western institutions and values throughout the world. This confidence was not based on any rational assessment of facts. The mania surrounding globalization was only the latest incarnation of the Enlightenment faith

23. Suman Guha Mozumdar, "Kishore Mahbubani", *India Abroad*, December 8, 2006, p. 14.

24. Ibid., p. 15.

> that the advance of science and technology would create a universal civilization. Predictably it was not long before it gave way to anxiety. Islamist terrorism and the emergence of Russia as an authoritarian great power, together with US troubles in Iraq, have shattered the certainties of the 1990s. Yet the faith they expressed has not been destroyed. In its most influential forms the Enlightenment has always been an ersatz religion — think of Marxism, for example — and in response to the shocks of the past years it has undergone a fundamentalist revival in much the same way that other faiths have done.[25]

He goes on to say:

> Will Hutton, among these revivalists, in his new book reveals another source of the Enlightenment's renewed popularity — the mounting panic induced by the rise of China. On the first page of *The Writing on the Wall* he asks anxiously: "Is the baton of global leadership going to pass from Anglo-Saxon hands, which held so many values in common, to Chinese hands? If so, the implications could not be more profound. The world would have to accommodate a wholly different civilization and values; the character of global institutions, our culture and the primacy of our English language would be challenged."
>
> For Hutton this prospect is unthinkable, and he goes on at once to declare that "if the next century is going to be Chinese, it will only be because China embraces the economic and political pluralism of the West in general, and our Enlightenment institutions in particular, modified, of course, for the Chinese experience." The caveat is worth noting. There is nothing about accepting China on equal terms with the West — rather, "our"

25. *Guardian Weekly*, February 2-8, 2007, p. 23.

> Enlightenment inheritance must be modified to ensure that China becomes Western.[26]

13. Sometimes universality or **universalism** is paired with **multiculturalism**.

    Upendra Baxi offers several remarks apropos the concerns of the book, while commenting on *The Ticklish Subject: The Absent Center of Political Ontology* (1999) by Slavoj Žižek. He frames these remarks in the broad context that, when it comes to the discourse of universal human rights, multiculturalism paradoxically concedes both "*too much* and *not enough*." He writes:

    > As concerns human rights, multiculturalism concedes both "*too much* and *not enough*." It tolerates the Other not as a real Other "but the ascetic of immigrants from the South to the North. Žižek's point however cuts deeper. The multiculturalists advance and applaud the progressive abolition of capital punishment as a kind of (Parsonian) evolutionary universal of human rights; on the other hand, they remain "tolerant of the most brutal violations of human rights" lest they be accused of preferred (White) value imposition. The Other needs fuller recognition: on the one hand, in terms of "cultural *jouissance* that even a "victim" can find in a practice of another culture that appears cruel and barbaric to us" (here, of course, Talal Asad, to whom I refer later, is a more insightful guide than Žižek), and on the other hand, in terms of the split in the Other (a point I have been making under different phrase-regime so far). In the latter situation, reference to human rights (presumably defined by the West, and on this point Žižek is still Eurocentric as concerns the site of the origins of human rights!), as a

---

26. *Guardian Weekly*, February 2-8, 2007, p. 23.

> catalyst sets in motion an authentic protest against the constraints of one's own culture.[27]

On the one hand, Baxi is able to compliment Žižek as follows: "Žižek brings valuable correctives to the current conceptions of multiculturalism generally, and their implications on human rights in particular. Neither takes seriously new modes of social reproduction of globalized coloniality nor alerts us so fully to the empty potential of multiculturalism as a culture of no cultures. A reminder of epistemic racism always renders great service to the future of human rights."[28] On the other hand, he is also constrained to observe:

> Yet the examples that guide Žižek remain problematic, whether progressive abolition of capital punishment as merely constituting a "Western" evolutionary indicator (*as if* traditions such as Hinduism, Buddhism, Confucianism, or indigenous religions had no space in the denial of retribution of this magnitude) or clitoridectomy as a pathway to "feminine dignity," even as a form of "victim" cultural *jouissance*. Traditions, as well as critiques, of multi-cultural theory and practices will cause anxiety across the North-South divide on the universality of human rights.[29]

Upendra Baxi also adds a wrinkle to his view that multiculturalism concedes both too much and not enough in relation to human rights, when he returns to this point and writes as follows:

> The point, from a human rights perspective, is simply that extremes of *too much* and *not enough* remain constructed, in the final analysis, from the perspective of

27. Upendra Baxi, op. cit., p. 110.
28. Ibid., p. 111.
29. Ibid.

progressive Eurocentrism with all its contradictions. Were the subaltern ever to speak, its Other will be the split Euro-American postmodern "absent" subject![30]

14. Yet another distinction which might be important to draw in the context of universality may turn on whether a **universal idea** is **universally upheld**.

This point emerges from the following remarks by Willard G. Oxtoby, who writes:

> Do all peoples have a sense of the oneness of humanity? This is an interesting question, since the idea of a universal humanity may not necessarily be universally held. All cultures, it would seem, distinguish human beings from animals — from the "other" animals, perhaps we should say. It is not so clear that every culture is interested in the totality of the human race to quite the same extent. The anthropologist Kenelm Burridge, in *Encountering Aborigines* (1973), a book devoted to the specific case of Australian aboriginal cultures, makes the provocative point that European culture has shown an openness to, and curiosity about, other cultures that is unusual and perhaps even unique. If Burridge is right, then cosmopolitanism may still have an unfinished job ahead to establish itself more firmly in the world.[31]

A similar tension between what is held to be universally true, at least in principle, but not universally accepted in practice, can be detected in the following statement about religions, specially towards the end, in which an attempt is made to distil the missionary spirit.

---

30. Ibid., p. 111.

31. Willard G. Oxtoby, *The Meaning of Other Faiths*, Philadelphia: The Westminster Press, 1983, pp. 58-59. The point made by Kenelm Burridge is supported by Bernard Lewis, *Islam and the West*, New York: Oxford University Press, 1993, pp. 123-24.

> The first point is that they all seem to be impelled by a unique revelation or a great discovery about the nature of being and existence, the discovery of which prompts a momentous personal transformation and a revitalization of social and cultural purpose given by an awareness of transcendence that brings spiritual and moral renewal. This generates a salvific metaphysical-moral vision that is not only of intense personal meaning but also thought to be of universal import for humanity. This vision induces a passion that intellectually, morally and emotionally is felt by those grasped by it from magical practices of local deities and cults, from familial, clan, caste, or ethnic loyalties, from feeble or dysfunctional political-economic conditions, and from "meaningless" or ineffective rites and rituals. The missionary impulse that grows from this source becomes "homeless", for it finds its true home in a realm that relativizes all that is understood to be natural or conventional, which it then tries either to escape or to transform. *It further evokes a desire to bring about the universal acceptance and application of the vision, which it holds to be universally true in principle, even if it is not universally accepted.*[32]

15. Another term with which the word universalism is sometimes paired is imperialism, particularly in a context in which the practice of **religious universalism** is felt to be tainted by **cultural imperialism**. Max Stackhouse has however drawn attention to two factors which help differentiate universal, that is, missionary expansion from cultural imperialism. According to him, the "imperialist understands the message only in terms of its socio-cultural

---

32. Max L. Stackhouse, "Missions: Missionary Activity", in Lindsay Jones, editor in chief, *Encyclopedia of Religion* (second edition), Farmington Hills, MI: Thomson Gale, 2005, vol. 9, p. 6069, emphasis supplied.

trappings in highly particularistic ways," whereas "the true religious missionary recognizes a distinction between the message and the accoutrements, the universalistic kernel and the incidental husk."[33] He cites the following cases as illustrative of imperialism rather than universalism:

> Imperialism obtains when, for example, Buddhism in Myanmar becomes identical with and a tool of the Burman peoples as opposed to those of the Chin, Kachin, or other Burmese peoples; when Christianity becomes "Aryanized" in the Nazi period or sanctifies apartheid as in South Africa; when Islam in, for instance, Malaysia, Iran, or Saudi Arabia is understood to be coterminous with the fate of the countries themselves; or when Communism is thought to be identical with "socialism in one country" and celebrated with a personality cult.[34]

The second way of distinguishing between the two is also best explained in his own words:

> Second, missionary activity is rooted in the fundamental assumptions that, once people are exposed to "the truth" that has been proclaimed, they will choose this truth and that they ought to be free to encounter and choose even "foreign" truth. Missions presuppose that a truly universalistic vision is convincing to the mind, compelling to the will, and attractive to the heart. Missions thus require, or provoke, a situation in which freedom of thought, choice, and affection can create new communities of conviction to celebrate and exercise what the will, mind and heart have come to hold dear. However, much missionary activity has been carried out hand in hand with cultural arrogance, military power and economic opportunism. There has been and remains in

33. Ibid., p. 6071.

34. Ibid.

> principle a sharp tension between missionary efforts and imperialistic imposition of religion by force or "mind control", a fact increasingly documented by missiologists examining the relative validity of the charge that missions are but the ideological instruments of colonial practice. Those incapable of imagining a fundamental transformation of thought, disposition, and loyalty by conversion to a new religious insight, however, always attribute the change to nefarious interests.[35]

16. Another word with which **universalism** could be paired is **universism**, a term used by J.J.M. de Groot to describe Taoist, Confucian and Shintō cultures where the religious life "is one of harmony with both the natural and human orders, a submersion of individuality in an organic relationship and in an inwardly experienced oneness with it."[36] This sense has more to do with how one relates to the universe around oneself than with the universal, or that element which permeates all the individual representations of it. The universalism of human rights discourse, in this sense, could be mildly disruptive of universism, in the sense that it emphasizes the individual both against the community and the natural world, or has been alleged to, at least until recently.

IV

The foregoing survey was intended to open up the question of universality and to identify some of the distinctions which a concept of universality must negotiate in order to be

35. Ibid.

36. Winsten L. King, "Religion (First Edition)", in Lindsay Jones, editor-in-chief, *Encyclopedia of Religion* (second edition), Farmington Hills, MI: Thomson & Gale, 2005, vol. 11, p. 7692.

considered viable. One particular distinction, out of the many distinctions drawn in the course of the discussion, seems to be particularly relevant in the present context. The distinction is hard to articulate but can be sensed in the way the **universal** may differ from the **unified**, or in the gap by which a universal idea falls short of being universally upheld (as when one notes that "the idea of a universal humanity may not necessarily be universally held"[37]), or in the distinction between two senses of **universal scripture** (when that expression might mean either that **one** particular scripture is accepted by all the world religions or that all the world religions possess **one** scripture of their own).

The pitfalls of "universalism" in universalist human rights discourse are highlighted, if attention is drawn to those areas of the application of human rights, where its claim to universalism seems to be on the verge of generating serious problems in theory and practice. Two examples in practice and then two theoretical examples are offered below to illustrate this point.

1. One area where such universalism seems to be potentially problematical is that of family life. Let us take the question of the wellbeing of children as a case in point. Let us suppose that one identifies a family in which children are being treated in a less than ideal manner. The usual question people will ask the parents in such a situation is, "Don't you love your children?" If this fails they are likely to exhort the family to do its duty by the children. When even this fails, they are likely to begin speaking in terms of the rights of the children, and when things really get out of hand, they may alert the authorities.

---

37. Willard G. Oxtoby, *The Meaning of Other Faiths*, Philadelphia: The Westminster Press, 1983, p. 58.

It is important to identify these three stages and subject them to analysis. Note that in the first case — the appeal to love — the point of appeal is the individual's own conscience and the family unit as such of which one is a member, ideally held together by the glue of affection. In the second case — of appeal to duty — the appeal is still to the individual's conscience but two additional features are worth noting. Love discourse has been replaced by the sterner duty discourse and an outside agency — in the form of pastoral counselling — could also be involved in the situation by the well-wisher of the children. In the third case — the appeal to rights — this process of externalization is carried further. The appeal now is based on enforceable rights. The appeal is legal rather than moral or pastoral — and the State is brought into the picture. With love the corresponding unit was the family, with duty, in a manner of speaking, the church (although it is possible that the church could also have been brought into the situation earlier). With rights the corresponding unit is the State. There is some overgeneralization involved in the statement but one hopes the point is made.

The point now needs to be followed up. The concept of human rights was developed essentially in the context of the relationship of the individual with the State, not his family or church. It is true that it has implications for these — but the basic context was provided by the State. This basic context is now being extended to the home, when we talk of children's rights. It may well be that this is necessary because the families are failing in their duty. But it is one thing to do something out of necessity and another to do it out of choice.

One fears for the loss of these distinctions when rights discourse becomes the dominant moral idiom of our times. In other words — the application of rights discourse to children *out of choice* may represent an overextension of this discourse — an overuniversalization if you wish.

Perhaps history could serve as an early warning system here. In medieval times, theology overextended itself into the scientific realm with unhappy consequences; in our own times scientific discourse may be overextending itself into the Humanities — at least some think so — with the danger that the weight of Mozart's piano may become a subject of greater interest than his music, just because it is quantifiable. One exaggerates but hopes the point is made. Are we facing a similar danger in the moral realm? This is the first of the promised examples of what might be a case of overuniversalization of human rights in practice.

2. The second example is presented by what is now being called globalization. This process is probably not directly connected with human rights discourse, but to the extent that it is seen going hand in hand with the democratization process and with other developments one associates with a human rights regime, perhaps we are not out of line in including globalization in our discussion.

   Globalization as a process is capitalistic in nature. The overuniversalization of capitalism under the cover of human rights is the danger one needs to pay heed to here.

   The point may be elaborated as follows. Why, one might ask, is globalization, or capitalism for that matter, a danger? Those who object to globalization often draw attention to its negative economic and socio-political consequences, but one must tackle the topic ideologically.

The two great economic systems which characterized the last century were capitalism and communism. What is the crucial difference between the two from a broadly humanistic perspective? The following suggestion may have much to recommend in it — that communism or socialism tried to protect society against the worst, while capitalism tried to propel it towards the most, if not the best. Thus typically, communist countries provided assured employment, widespread medical care, etc. but not the highest standard of living. The capitalist countries aimed at providing the highest standard of living — but fell short at the other end of the spectrum, at least for some of the citizens. To the extent that human rights discourse is identified with *democratic* capitalism, globalization potentially remains another area of the overuniversalization of human rights, in the sense that in its relentless self-absorption the discourse may be willing to sacrifice human welfare at the altar of human rights, just as sometimes religion has been trampled upon in the name of religion.

3. Modern human rights discourse has been able to avoid many a dilemma by working primarily with the concepts of *individual* and *universal rights*, and by largely sidestepping the issue of group rights. This is because the categories of the individual and the universal dovetail neatly, as in the statement: everyone is unique. Some are *not* more unique than others: to be equal one does not have to be the same. All can thus be equal before the law without being the same.

   But members of a group have to be the *same* in some respect in order to be equal members of the group. This violates the universality principle of uniqueness.

Such a "grouped uniqueness" over and above individual uniqueness need not necessarily be problematic in human rights discourse provided it is temporary. If we were — all of us — the residents of a town and all our houses were swept away in a flash flood, we as a group would acquire "grouped uniqueness". The government will be able to sanction special aid for us without incurring the charge of favouritism, because our "grouped uniqueness" is adventitious and temporary and only lasts till our houses are rebuilt.

It is when such "grouped uniqueness" becomes persistent, instead of being transient, that we have a problem; that is, it is when it retains a defining characteristic over time — over a long period of time — or is such as cannot be overlooked as when based on colour, that it becomes a problem, specially when it becomes correlated with a disadvantage. Hence the significance of the "melting pot" — it was able to dissolve these grouped distinctions in a way and up to a point where this *group uniqueness* was ultimately reduced into becoming only an element of *individual uniqueness*.

Thus groups do not cause lasting problems for the individualistic and universalistic discourse of human rights so long as these groupings are essentially temporary in principle and practice, as in the example cited earlier, where helping a group of people who have lost their homes arouses no resentment. Similarly, when group identity dissolves over generations and becomes individualized, it does not cause serious problems. Problems arise when group identity is *permanently* based on birth, as in the classic understanding of caste. It is not enough for it to be based on birth alone. The fact that we are a human being is also based on birth; it is the membership of *another* group (other than humanity) based on birth which challenges this *universal* ascription — but only if the challenge is considered permanent.

Women as a group provide a useful illustration here. Thus to the extent that women claim rights as women who are human beings, rather than as human beings who are women, we will have to deal with group rights. By insisting that women's rights must be *subsumed* under human rights instead of being *incorporated* into it, is human rights offering us an example of overuniversalization? This is a moot point. The intention at the moment is only to raise it, not to answer it.

4. Let us deal with the simple statement that *everyone is unique*. This statement is itself fraught with tension if we pause long enough to detect it. It claims to be a universal statement: everyone is . . . but if everyone is unlike everyone else, then this is a peculiar kind of universal statement. It points to unity *without* uniformity. So what it really comes down to being is a statement of *unity* in diversity. We are all human beings, and at the same time unique.

   One may carry this point beyond the level of semantic curiosity with the help of Hindu ethics. Hindu ethics lays down two sets of rules of conduct — those which apply to us as belonging to a particular section of the population (class or *varṇa*) and as belonging to a particular cohort of the population (state of life or *āśrama*). This is the celebrated concept of *varṇāśrama dharma*: the appropriate code of conduct keeping one's membership of a class and one's age in mind. Thus a warrior in the stage of leading a family life is called upon to fight. However, Hindu ethics also provides for *sādhāraṇa dharma*, or a code of conduct to be pursued by people of all classes and in all stages of life. A little reflection allows us to rephrase this same concept as involving a code one may follow *irrespective* of one's class and stage of life, for that is what it is if it must be followed by all *varṇas* and in all *āśramas*. One such *dharma* or rule of conduct is non-violence.

Now what is one to do as a soldier whose specific or unique *dharma* calls upon him to kill but whose universal *dharma* calls on him to be non-violent. One need not pursue this important and much-discussed dilemma further here. One only needs to recognize that such a dilemma exists. Hindu ethics recognizes this as a *genuine* dilemma. What does one mean by calling it a genuine dilemma? What one means to say is that it might be beyond the powers of either fideism or rationalism to resolve it in an a priori way. That is to say: if fideism believes that with enough faith we will be able to find solutions to *all* moral dilemmas, and if rationalism believes that with enough reason we will similarly be able to find solutions to *all* moral dilemmas, then Hinduism says that this may not be possible in an a priori way. Which is to say that these dilemmas could not, at least not all of them, be resolved without regard to *their own specific* parameters.

The point which emerges from this is that the uniqueness of life will always cause problems for universalism — and human rights discourse perhaps will be no exception to this. The uniqueness of all human beings means that we must expect the unexpected to keep surfacing in human rights discourse. In other words, the tendency towards overuniversalization may well represent something we must constantly guard against in human rights discourse, when such discourse claims to be based on rationalism.

Everyone tends to be in favour of harmony, except perhaps some Marxists, but the jarring notes will only render the eventual harmony sweeter. These jarring notes consist of the points which problematize our current discourse on human rights. One may not wish to claim yet that they constitute aporias, but they do seem to be issues that require reflection in the context of the claim to universality made on behalf of human rights.

2

Is The Notion of Human Rights a Western Concept?[1]

Raimundo Panikkar

WE should approach this topic with great fear and respect. It is not a merely "academic" issue. Human rights are trampled upon in the East as in the West, in the North as in the South of our planet. Granting the part of the human greed and sheer evil in this universal transgression, could it not also be that human rights are not observed because in their present form they do not represent a universal symbol powerful enough to elicit understanding and agreement?

No culture, tradition or religion can today speak for the whole of humankind, let alone solve its problems. Dialogue and intercourse leading to a mutual fecundation are necessary. But sometimes the very conditions for dialogue are not given, because there are unspoken conditions which most partners cannot meet. It is a fact that the present-day formulation of human rights is the fruit of a very partial

---

1. This paper is an expanded and revised version of the presentation at the "Entretiens de Dakar", Senegal, to the annual session of the Institut International de Philosophie on *Philosophical Foundations of Human Rights*, a summary of which will appear in the Proceedings.

dialogue among the cultures of the world. It is only recently that this question has been acutely felt.[2]

I shall not enter into the details of the history of human rights, nor into an analysis of their nature. I shall confine myself to the interrogation implied in the title:

Are Human Rights a Universal Invariant?

The Method of Inquiry

DIATOPICAL HERMENEUTICS

It is claimed that human rights are universal. This alone entails a major philosophical query. Does it make sense to ask about conditions of universality when the very question about conditions of universality is far from universal? Philosophy can no longer ignore this inter-cultural problematic. Can we extrapolate the concept of human rights, from the context of the culture and history in which it was conceived, into a globally valid notion? Could it at least *become* a universal symbol? Or is it only one particular way of expressing — and saving — the *humanum?*

Although the question posed in the title is a legitimate one, there is something disturbing in this formulation as it was given to me. At least at first glance, it would seem to

2. Cf. probably the first Symposium of its kind convened by UNESCO at Bangkok in December 1979, *Meeting of Experts on the Place of Human Rights in Cultural and Religious Traditions*, where nine major schools of religious thought discussed the issue and recognized "that many of them have not paid sufficient attention to human rights . . . (and that) it is a task for the different religions of the world to deepen and eventually to enlarge and/or reformulate the urgent and important issue of human rights." (S 116 g of the Final Report SS79/CONF. 607/10 of 6 February, 1980). The entire report is worth reading.

offer only one alternative: either the notion of Universal Human Rights is a Western notion, or it is not. If it is, besides being a tacit indictment against those who do not possess such a valuable concept, its introduction into other cultures, even if necessary, would appear as a plain imposition from outside. It would appear, once again, as a continuation of the colonial syndrome, namely the belief that the constructs of one particular culture (God, Church, Empire, Western civilization, Science, Modern Technology, etc.) have, if not the monopoly, at least the privilege of possessing a universal value which entitles them to be spread all over the earth. If not, that is, if the concept of Universal Human Rights is not exclusively a Western concept, it would be difficult to deny that many a culture has let it slumber, thus again giving rise to an impression of the indisputable superiority of Western culture. There is nothing wrong in admitting a hierarchy of cultures, but this hierarchical order cannot be assumed as the starting point, nor can one side alone lay down the criteria necessary for establishing such a hierarchy. There is then a prior question implied by asking whether the notion of human rights is a Western concept. It is the question regarding the very nature of human rights, and it directly submits this notion to cross-cultural scrutiny.

Our question is a case in point of *diatopical hermeneutics*: the problem is how, from the *topos* of one culture, to understand the constructs of another.[3] It is wrong-headed methodology

---

3. By diatopical hermeneutics I understand a thematic reflection on the fact that the loci (topoi) of historically unrelated cultures make it problematic to understand one tradition with the tools of another, and the hermeneutical attempt to bridge such gulfs. Cf. R. Panikkar, *Myth, Faith and Hermeneutics*, New York, Paulist Press, 1979, p. 8 sq.

to begin by asking: Does another culture also have the notion of human rights? — assuming that such a notion is absolutely indispensable to guarantee human dignity. No question is neutral, for every question conditions its possible answers.

THE HOMEOMORPHIC EQUIVALENT

I was once asked to give the Sanskrit equivalents of the twenty-five key Latin words supposed to be emblematic of Western culture. I declined, on the grounds that which is the foundation of one culture need not be the foundation for another. Meanings are not transferable here. Translations are more delicate than heart transplants. So what must we do? We must dig down to where a homogenous soil or a similar problematic appears; we must search out the *homeomorphic equivalent* — to the concept of human rights in this case. "Homeomorphism is not the same as analogy; it represents a peculiar functional equivalence discovered through a topological transformation." It is "a kind of existential functional analogy."[4]

Thus we are not seeking merely to transliterate human rights into other cultural languages, nor should we be looking for mere analogies; we try instead to find the homeomorphic equivalent. If, for instance, human rights are considered to be the basis for the exercise of and respect for human dignity, we should investigate how another culture satisfies the equivalent need — and this can be done only once a common ground (a mutually understandable language) has been

4. Cf. R. Panikkar, *The Intrareligious Dialogue*, New York, Paulist Press, 1978, p.xxii. The two words *Brahman* and God, for instance, are neither analogous nor merely equivocal (nor univocal, of course). They are not exactly equivalent either. They are homeomorphic. They perform a certain type of respectively corresponding function in the two different traditions where these words are alive.

worked out between the two cultures. Or perhaps we should ask how the idea of a just social and political order could be formulated within a certain culture, and investigate whether the concept of human rights is a particularly appropriate way of expressing this order. A traditional Confucian might see this problem of order and rights as a question of "good manners" or in terms of his profoundly ceremonial or ritual conception of human intercourse, in terms of *li*. A Hindu might see it another way, and so on.

* * *

In order to clarify the question of our title, I shall indicate some of the assumptions on which the notion of human rights is based and immediately insert some cross-cultural reflections which will lead us to the *locus* — the context — of the question and the justification for my answer, which I would like to anticipate by means of a simile: Human rights are one window through which one particular culture envisages a just human order for its individuals. But those who live in that culture do not see the window. For this they need the help of another culture which sees through another window. Now I assume that the human landscape as seen through the one window is both similar to and different from the vision of the other. If this is the case, should we smash the windows and make of the many portals a single gaping aperture — with the consequent danger of structural collapse — or should we enlarge the viewpoints as much as possible and, most of all, make people aware that there are — and have to be — a plurality of windows? This latter option would be the one in favour of a healthy pluralism. This is much more than a merely academic question. There can be no serious talk about cultural pluralism without a genuine socio-economic-political pluralism. This is, for example, what has led intellectual groups in India to ask whether "civil rights" are not incompatible with "economic rights." At any rate, to speak of cultural pluralism within what could be called a paneconomic ideology makes little sense and amounts to treating the other cultures of the world as mere folklore. The example of the notion of *dharma* from the Indian tradition will offer us a point of reference from which to formulate our conclusion.

Assumptions and Implications of the Western Concept

I take the expression "human rights" in the sense of the Universal Declaration of Human Rights adopted by the General Assembly of the United Nations in 1948.[5] The Western, mainly liberal protestant roots of the Human Rights Declaration are well known.[6] The Western world has known of the struggle for citizen's rights since the Middle Ages.[7] This struggle for

5. I shall capitalize Human Rights when these words have the particular meaning derived from this "Universal Declaration."

6. The dates to recall are:

   10 December 1948 — Proclamation in Paris of the Universal Declaration;

   4 November 1950 — Adoption in Rome of the Convention safeguarding Human Rights and fundamental freedom, known as "The European Convention on Human Rights";

   20 March 1952 — Adoption in Paris of the first additional Protocol to this Convention; and

   16 December 1966 — International Covenant on Civil and Political Rights; Optional Protocol (to the latter — not passed unanimously).

7. For the astounding documents of the first nine Christian centuries, cf. the collection and translation with insightful introduction by H. Rainer, *Kirche und Staat*, Munich, Kosel, 1961. The first edition in 1943 during the Second World →

concrete rights, rooted in the practices and value systems of a particular nation or country, is felt with greater urgency after the French Revolution.[8] Western man passes from a corporate belonging in a community of blood, work and historical destiny, based on practically accepted custom and theoretically acknowledged authority, to a society based on impersonal law and ideally free contract, to the modern State, for which explicitly rational norms and duties are required. The problem becomes increasingly acute with the growth of individualism.

→ War with the title *Abenlandische Kirchenfeihiet*, is in itself a document for Human Rights.

Because it is less known than the *Magna Carta* of King John of England in 1215, let us mention King Alfonso IX of Leon in 1188 with his rights to life, honour, home and property.

Interesting also is the statement and justification of Francisco de Victoria in 1538: "Cuando los subditos tengan conciencia de la injusticia de la guerra, no les es licito ir a ella, *sea que se equivoquen o no*" (emphasis mine). *De los indios o del derech de la guerra*, II, 23 (Ed. BAC, Madrid 1960, p. 831). ("When its subjects are aware of the injustice of a war, it is not lawful for them to go to it, *whether they are in error or not.*") And the reason he gives is to quote Rom. XIV, 23: "omne quod non est ex fide peccatum est," which he translates "todo lo que no es segun conciencia es peccado" (ibid., emphasis added). The Pauline passage is usually rendered: "Whatever does not come from faith is sin." Victoria's variation reads: "Whatever is not in accordance with one's *conscience* is a sin." Cf. the Thomistic principle that the rational being that is Man has to follow his or her personal conscience in order to act morally.

8. Just as a memorandum, we may recall:

1689 – Bill of Rights (England)

1776 – Virginia Bill of Rights

1789 – (26 August) – Déclaration des droits de l'homme at du citoyen

1798 – American Bill of Rights

This paper assumes knowledge of the history of human rights, as well as of the fact that this transition from one form of collective life to another more modern form is said today to have acquired a worldwide character. We would like to concentrate on the more strictly philosophical *assumptions* which seem to be at the basis of the declaration.

1. At the basis of the discourse on human rights there is the assumption of a *universal human nature* common to all peoples. Otherwise, a Universal Declaration could not legally have been proclaimed. This idea in its turn is connected with the old notion of a Natural Law.

   But the contemporary Declaration of Human Rights further *implies*:

   (a) that this human nature must be *knowable*. For it is one thing to accept human nature uncritically or mythically, and another to know it. Otherwise, the declaration could not speak and legislate about Rights that are universal;

   (b) that this human nature is known by means of an equally universal organ of knowledge, generally called *reason*. Otherwise, if its knowledge should depend on a special intuition, revelation faith, decree of a prophet or the like, human rights could not be taken as *natural* rights — inherent in Man. This must be a commonly-held knowledge. Otherwise human rights could not be declared universal by an Assembly which does not claim to have a privileged epistemological status. This is made plain by the use of the word "declaration", which stresses the fact that it is not an imposition from above but a public explication, a making clear of what is inherent in the very nature of Man;[9] and

(c) that this human nature is essentially *different* from the rest of reality. Other living beings inferior to Man obviously have no human rights, and creatures superior to Man are likely not to exist. Man is the master of himself and the universe. He is the supreme legislator on Earth – the question of whether a Supreme Being exists or not remains open, but ineffective.[10]

2. The second assumption is that of the *dignity of the individual.* Each individual is, in a certain sense, absolute, irreducible to another. This is probably the major thrust of the modern question of human rights. Human rights defend the dignity of the individual *vis-à-vis* Society at large, and the State in particular.

But this in turn implies:

(a) not only the distinction but also the *separation* between individual and society. In this view the human being

---

9. The Paris document is a *declaration,* a manifest statement making clear what is already there, an explication (*declarare,* to make clear — from *dē-clārāre.* Cf. *clārus,* clear, but also loud *(clamor)*). It is not a law, a superimposition, a human creation. But the recognition or discovery of something intrinsic to the nature of the thing; in this case "the inherent dignity and equal and inalienable rights of all the members of the human family," as the Preamble to the 1948 Declaration says.

10. This practical a-theism and even practical ignorance of any ulterior philosophical issue or religious factor became patent in the presentation and discussion of the Bangkok Conference mentioned above, let alone in the more official meetings where Philosophy and Religion have hardly a voice.

is fundamentally the individual. Society is a kind of superstructure, which can easily become a menace and also an alienating factor for the individual. Human rights are there primarily to protect the individual;

(b) The *anatomy* of humankind *vis-à-vis* and often versus the Cosmos. This is clearly shown in the ironic ambivalence of the English expression, which means at the same time *"Menschenrechte", "droits de l'Homme," and also "menschliche Recht", "droits humains"* (human rights). The Cosmos is a kind of understructure. The individual stands in between Society and World. Human rights defend the autonomy of the human individual; and

(c) Resonances of the idea of Man as *microcosmos* and reverberations of the conviction that Man is *imago dei*, and at the same time the relative independence of this conviction from ontological and theological formulations. The individual has an inalienable dignity because he is an end in himself and a kind of absolute. You can cut off a finger for the sake of an entire body, but can you kill one person to save another?[11]

3. The third assumption is that of a *democratic social order*. Society is assumed to be not a hierarchical order founded on a divine will or law or mythical origin, but a sum of "free" individuals organized to achieve otherwise

11. Cf. R. Panikkar, "Singularity and Individuality: The Double Principle of Individuation." *Revue international de philosophie* XIX, 1-2, No, 111-12 (1975) pp. 141-66, where it is argued that the ontic status of human individuals is basically different from that of all other individual entities; in short, that we cannot treat human individuals as we could peanuts or cattle, by a merely numerical individuality.

unreachable goals. Human rights, once again, serve mainly to protect the individual. Society here is not seen as a family or a protection, but as something unavailable which can easily abuse the power conferred on it (precisely by the assent of the sum of its individuals). This society crystallizes in the State, which theoretically expresses the will of the people, or at least of the majority. The idea of an Empire, or a People or a Nation with a transcendent destiny — whose duty it is to carry through the entrusted mission independent of the will of the members of that society — still exists today in some theocratic States, but even most of these try to palliate their messianic vocation by democratic endorsements.

This implies:

(a) that each individual is seen as equally important and thus equally responsible for the welfare of society. Hence the individual has the right to stand by his or her convictions and propagate them or to resist impositions against his or her inherent freedom;

(b) that Society is nothing but the sum total of the individuals whose wills are sovereign and ultimately decisive.[12] There is no instance superior to Society. Even if there were to exist a God or a superhuman Reality, this too would be filtered through human consciousness and human institutions; and

(c) that the rights and freedoms of the individual can be limited only when they impinge upon the rights and freedoms of other individuals, and in this way majority

12. "The will of the people shall be the basis of the authority of government", — Art. 21, 3 of the declaration.

rule is rationally justified.[13] And when the rights of an individual are curtailed by "reasons of State," this is allegedly justified by the fact that the State is supposed to embody the will and the interests of the majority. It is interesting to note that the "Universal Declaration" speaks of "freedoms" in the plural and, even more intriguing, of "fundamental freedoms." The individualization does not stop at the individual, but divides this segregated entity even further into separated freedoms.

In enumerating these Assumptions and Implications I do not mean to say that they were actually in the minds of the framers of the declaration. In fact, there is evidence to suggest that no unanimity could be found regarding the basis of the rights that were being declared. But the declaration clearly was articulated along the lines of the historical trends of the Western world during the last three centuries, and in tune with a certain philosophical anthropology or individualistic humanism which helped justify them.

Cross-Cultural Reflections

Is the concept of human rights a universal concept?

The answer is a plain *no*. Three reasons vouch for it.

(a) No concept as such is universal. Each concept is valid primarily where it was conceived. If we want to extend

13. "In the exercise of his rights and freedoms, everyone shall be subject only to such limitations as are determined by law solely for the purpose of securing due recognition and respect for the rights and freedoms of others and of meeting the *just* requirements of *morality*, *public order* and the general *welfare* in a *democratic* society." Art. 29, 2 (Emphasis of the problematic words added.)

its validity beyond its own context we shall have to justify the extrapolation. Even mathematical concepts imply the previous acknowledgement of a limited field defined by the axioms we postulate. Furthermore, every concept tends to be univocal. To accept the possibility of universal concepts, we would imply a strictly rationalistic conception of reality. But even if this were theoretically true, it would not be the actual case because *de facto* humankind presents a plurality of universal discourses. To accept this fact that the concept of human rights *is* not universal, does not yet mean that it should not become so. Now, in order to make the concept become universally valid, it should fulfil at least two conditions. First, it should, on the one hand, eliminate all the other contradictory concepts. This may seem improbable, but there is a logical necessity here and, theoretically, it would all be for the best. Second, it should be the universal point of reference for any problem regarding human dignity. In other words, it should displace all other homeomorphic equivalents and be the pivotal centre of a just social order. To put it in the other way, the culture which has given birth to the concept of human rights should also be called upon to become a universal culture. This may well be one of the causes of a certain uneasiness one senses in non-Western thinkers who study the question of human rights. They fear for the identity of their own cultures.

(b) Within the vast field of Western culture itself, the very assumptions which serve to situate our problems are not universally recognized. The particular origin of the formation of human rights is sufficiently well known. Probably the most important sources of dissent are three.[14]

(i) **Theology**: Human rights need to be grounded, says the theological view. In a superior, transcendent and unmanipulable value, those traditional symbols are God as origin and guarantor of both human rights and duties. Otherwise, they are only a political device in the hands of the powerful. According to this view, the declaration suffers from a naive optimism regarding the goodness and autonomy of human nature. Moreover, it implies a deficient anthropology, inasmuch as it seems to view the human person as merely a bundle of needs, material and psychology, of which it then proceeds to make an inventory.[15] And finally, in case of doubts and conflicts, who is going to decide? Majority rule is only a euphemism for the law of the jungle; the power of the strongest.

---

14. We do not include here a fourth source of dissent, namely the *political*, because the argument in such cases bears mainly on different interpretations of facts, emphases and factors other than those related to the nature of Human Rights. Cf. as a single example: *Colloques de Riyad, de Paris, du Vatican, de Genéve et de Strasbourg sur le dogme musulman et les droits de l'homme en Islam,* Riyad, Ministere de la Justice; Beirut, Dar Al Kitab Allubhani, 1974; and D. Sidorsky (ed.) *Essays on Human Contemporary Issues and Jewish Perspectives,* Philadelphia, The Jewish Publication Society of America, 1979.

15. "Human rights, in short, are statements of basic needs and interests." S.I. Benn, *The Encylopedia of Philosophy*, New York, Macmillan, 1967, *subvoce Rights*, speaking about the U.N. Declaration.

(ii) **Marxism:** For the Marxists, the human rights are merely *"Klassenrechte"*, the class rights.[16] "There are no rights without duties and no duties without rights." They reflect interests of a certain class and in many cases only its aspirations. There is no mention of the economic conditions for the effective realization of what are said to be universal human claims. Further, there is something abstract and too general about most of these rights; they are not sufficiently grounded in the material and cultural reality of particular groups. Finally, their individualism is evident. The individual is conceived as being in confrontation with (rather than included in) society, although the latter is said to be the result of freely contracting individuals. Society is not merely the sum total of individuals and it has the rights which the individual may not violate. History has transcendent power.

(iii) **History**: "Human rights" appear to some students of recent history as another example of the more or less conscious domination exerted by the powerful nations to maintain their privileges and defend the *status quo*. Human rights continues to be a political weapon. They were known long ago but only for the nobleman, for the free citizen, or for the male whites or Christians, etc. When they were hastily applied to "human beings", it was often defined just as groups belonging to the race who could properly be styled "human". If not all humans had human rights, the claim of human

---

16. Cf. K. Marx, *Zur Judenfrage* I, p. 352.

rights on behalf of animals, plants and things would seem and still do seem bizarre, not to say ridiculous, in spite of occasional remonstrances delivered by Societies for the Protection of Animals. Animals and the like have rights, but not like the human ones. And, as we have seen, this particular notion of the "human" has not always been very humane. And who is to speak for the whole? History discloses that only the victors declare and promulgate "rights", which are simply what the powerful consider right at any given time.

(c) From a cross-cultural stance, the problem appears exclusively Western, i.e. the question itself is at stake. Most of the assumptions and implications enumerated earlier are simply not given in other cultures. Furthermore, from a non-Western point of view, the problem itself is not seen as such so that it is not merely a question of agreeing or disagreeing with the answer. If anything, the experience is in a radically different way. A *diatopical* hermeneutic does not deal with just another point of view on the *same* problem. At issue here is not simply the answer, but the problem itself.

Now, is it possible to have access to other *topoi* so that we may be able to understand other cultures from within, i.e. as they understand themselves? We may not be able to jump over our own categories of understanding, but it may not be impossible to have one foot in one culture and the second in another. Generally, we have only one culture as we have only one mother-tongue — but we may also have a father-tongue. We cannot a priori deny this possibility. I recall that, in certain parts of the East, to be illiterate means to know only a single language. It is in dialogue with others that we can encompass our common ground. We may not integrate more than one culture in ourselves but we may open the possibility of a wider and deeper integration by opening ourselves, in dialogue, to others.

The following parallelism may be instructive. To assume that without the explicit recognition of human rights, life would be chaotic and have no meaning, belongs to the same order of ideas as to think that without the belief in one God as understood in the Abrahamic tradition human life would dissolve itself in total anarchy. This line of thinking leads to the belief that Atheists, Buddhists and Animists, for instance, should be considered as human aberrations. In the same vein: either human rights, or chaos. This attitude does not belong exclusively to Western culture. To call the stranger a barbarian is all too common an attitude among the peoples of the world. And, as we shall mention later, there is a legitimate and inbuilt claim to universality in any affirmation of truth. The problem is that we tend to identify the limits of our own vision with the human horizon.

CROSS-CULTURAL CRITIQUE

There are no trans-cultural values, for the simple reason that a value exists as such only in a given cultural context.[17] But there may be cross-cultural values, for which a critique is indeed possible. The latter does not consist in evaluating one cultural construct with the categories of another, but in trying to understand and criticize one particular human problem with the tools of understanding of the different cultures concerned,

---

17. "Keine Rechte ohne Pflichten, keine Pflichten ohne rechte," Marx-Engels, *Werke* XVI, 521 *apud* G. Klaus, M Buhr, *Philosophisches Wörterbuch*, Leipzig. VEB, 1976, *sub voce Menschenrecthe*.

and at the same time taking thematically into consideration that the very awareness and, much more, the formulation of the problem is already culturally bound. Our question is then to examine the possible cross-cultural value of the issue of human rights, an effort which begins by delimiting the cultural boundaries of the concept. The dangers of cultural West-centrism are only too patent today.

(a) We have already mentioned the particular historical origins of the Declaration of Human Rights. To claim universal validity of human rights in the formulated sense, implies the belief that most of the people of the world today are engaged in much the same way as the Western nations in a process of transition from more or less mythical *Gemeinschaften* (feudal principalities, self-governing cities, guilds, local communities, tribal institution . . .) to a "rationally" and "contractually" organized "modernity" as known to the Western industrialized world. This is a questionable assumption. No one can predict the evolution (or eventual disintegration) of those traditional societies which have started from different material and cultural bases and whose reaction to modern Western civilization may therefore follow hitherto unknown lines.

Further, the very powerful Declaration of Human Rights also shows its weakness from another point of view. Something has been lost when it has to be explicitly declared. As the Chinese say: It is when *yi* (justice) declines that *li* (ritual) arises.[18] Or as the British and Spaniards repeat: There are things which you take for granted and

18. Cf., R. Panikkar, "Aporias in the Comparative Philosophy of Religion," *Man in World*, XIII, 3-4 (1980), pp. 357-83.

about which you do not speak. And in some traditional societies, you cannot boast of being noble or a friend of the royal family because the very moment you do so, you lose your nobility and your friendship with the reigning house.[19] When human rights are declared, this is a sign that the very foundation on which they rest has already been weakened. The declaration only postpones the collapse. In traditional words, when the taboo of the sacred disappears, sacredness fades away. If you have to teach a mother to love her child, something is amiss with motherhood. Or, as some theoreticians of human rights have also recognized, the legislation on human rights is introduced in order to find a justification for contravening somebody else's freedom. Putting it positively, you need some justification to encroach on somebody's field of activity.

I am not saying this in order to revert to Utopian dreams of an earthly paradise, but just to sound another voice. You may promulgate laws, but you do not declare what is the case — unless it has ceased to be evident; you do not proclaim an "ought" if there are no transgressions at all.

(b) We may now briefly reconsider the three assumptions mentioned above. They may pass muster, insofar as they express an authentically valid human issue from one particular context. But the very context may be susceptible to a legitimate critique from the perspective of other cultures. To do this systematically would require that we choose one culture after another and examine the assumptions of the declaration in the light of each culture chosen. We shall limit ourselves here to token reflections

19. *Tao Te Ching*, p. 18.

under the very broad umbrella of a pre-Modern, non-Western state of mind.

(i) There is certainly a *universal human nature* but, first of all, this nature does not need to be segregated and fundamentally distinct from the nature of all living beings and/or the entire reality. Thus exclusively *human rights* would be seen as a violation of "cosmic rights" and an example of self-defeating anthropocentrism, a novel kind of apartheid. To retort that "cosmic rights" is a meaningless expression would only betray the underlying cosmology of the objection, for which the phrase makes no sense. But the existence of a different cosmology is precisely what is at stake here. We speak of the laws of nature; why not also of her rights?

Secondly, the interpretation of this "universal human nature," i.e. Man's self-understanding belongs equally to his human nature. Thus to single out one particular interpretation of it may be valid, but it is not universal and may not apply to the entirety of human nature.

Thirdly, to proclaim the undoubtedly positive concept of human rights may turn out to be a Trojan horse, surreptitiously introduced into other civilizations which will then all but be obliged to accept those ways of living, thinking and feeling for which human rights is the proper solution in cases of conflict. It is a little like the way technology is often introduced in many parts of the world: it is imported to solve the problems that it has itself created. We have already made reference to this when criticizing the universalization of the concept of Indigenous human rights.

(ii) Nothing could be more important than to underscore and defend the *dignity of the human person*. But the person should be distinguished from the individual. The individual is just an abstraction, i.e. a selection of a few aspects of the other person for practical purposes. My *person*, on the other hand, is also in "my" parents, children, friends, foes, ancestors and successors. "My" person is also in "my" ideas and feelings and in "my" belongings. If you hurt "me," you are equally damaging my whole clan, and possibly yourself as well. Rights cannot be individualized in this way. Is it the right of the mother, or the child? — in the case of abortion. Or perhaps of the father and relatives as well? Rights cannot be abstracted from duties; the two are correlated. The dignity of the human person may equally be violated by your language, or by your desecrating a place I consider holy, even though it does not "belong" to me in the sense of individualized private property. You may have "bought" it for a sum of money, while it belongs to me by virtue of another order altogether. An individual is an isolated knot; a person is the entire fabric around the knot, woven from the total fabric of the real. The limits to a person are not fixed, they depend utterly on his or her personality. Certainly without the knots the net would collapse; but without the net, the knots would not even exist.

To aggressively defend my individual rights, for instance, may have negative, i.e. unjust, repercussions on others and perhaps even on myself. The need for consensus in many traditions — instead of majority opinion — is based precisely on the corporate nature of human rights.

A paragraph on language is required here. Each language has its own genius and its own particular way to see the world and even to be it and be in it. But from a cross-cultural perspective, each language has to show the flexibility necessary to incorporate other human experiences. I know that in current English "individual" is synonymous with "person", but this should not prevent me from using these two words in the sense I have suggested, and from recognizing a particular human trend which tends to identify the human being with the most salient features of a gross "individualized" body or at least to inscribe it within that framework. In drawing the distinction between individual and person I would put much more content in it than a French moral philosophy would do nowadays, for instance. I would like to adduce this case as a particular instance of two radically different anthropologies.

(iii) *Democracy* is also a great value and infinitely better than any dictatorship. But it amounts to tyranny to put the peoples of the world under the alternative of choosing either democracy or dictatorship. Human rights are tied to democracy. Individuals need to be protected when the structure which is above them (Society, the State or the Dictator — by whatever name) is not qualitatively superior to them, i.e. when it does not belong to a higher order. Human rights is a legal device for the protection of smaller numbers of people (the minority or the individual) faced with the power of greater numbers. This implies a quantitative reductionism; the person is reduced to the individual and the individual to the basis of society. I may put it more positively by saying that it is the way by which the individual as cornerstone of society is protected, and his or her dignity recognized. In a hierarchical concept of reality, the particular human being cannot defend his or her rights by demanding or exacting them independently of the whole. The wounded order has to be set straight again, or it has to change altogether. Other traditional societies have different means to more or less successfully restore the order. The king may fail in his duty to protect the people, but will a Declaration of Human Rights be a corrective unless it also has the power to constrain the king? Can a democracy be imposed and remain democratic?[20]

The policy of non-alignment subscribed to by many countries of Africa and Asia here strikes a much deeper chord than possible political opportunism, or just another way of being relevant in the contemporary political scene. It represents precisely this refusal to admit the vision of the world as a function of the just-mentioned set of dilemmas represented by the so-called superpowers.

In short, the cross-cultural critique does not invalidate the Declaration of Human Rights, but offers new perspectives for an internal criticism and sets the limits of validity of human rights, offering at the same time both possibilities for enlarging its realm, if the context changes, and of a mutual fecundation with other conceptions of Man and Reality.

20. The *Mānavadharmaśāstra* (2-4) puts the same idea in a more sophisticated way: To act from a desire for reward is reprehensible. Yet without that desire, no action is possible. Laws are needed to put order into those human actions.

Should the Symbol of Human Rights be a Universal Symbol?

It should be noted that I speak here of human rights as a symbol which, unlike a concept, is by its nature polyvalent and polysemic.

The answer is yes, and no.

(a) **Yes.** When a culture as a whole discovers certain values as ultimate, these values must have a certain universal meaning. Only collective and culturally expressed universal values may be said to be human values. A mere private value cannot be called a *human* value. It is a humane value, but not necessarily a value for every human — as *human rights* claims to be. As a matter of fact, human rights come as a corrective to the former exclusive rights of the whites, the Believers, the Rich, the Brahmins and others — without meaning to touch legitimate privileges in the traditional sense of the word. The declaration of human rights needs to be considered, at least in its intention, as a declaration with universal validity. To say that human rights are not universal would amount to saying that they are not human; they would cease to be *human rights.* The whole novelty of the declaration lies precisely here, in the assertion that every human being, by the mere fact of being human, is endowed with inalienable rights that everybody should respect.

In that sense we may have here something rather unique and revolutionary in the Declaration of Human Rights. Here indeed we have the positive side of the individual *vis-à-vis* the person. Every single human being in its individuality, by the very fact of being born, has a dignity and rights equal to any other. It is not one's place in society, or degree of civilization, or intellect, more or religious endowments that counts. Certainly, limits will immediately appear; you may be subnormal or abnormal, and not only physically, but also morally — or, others would also add, intellectually or religiously. But the naked fact of being born is the universal symbol on which human rights is based. From this point of view, the claim to universality of human rights has found a solid basis.

Paradoxically enough, the Christian origin of this belief has been the cause of some of its degradation, i.e. when it became an ideology, a doctrine to serve the interests of one particular group. Everybody is born free and equal; all human beings are equal in the sight of God; every human person has the same rights as any other. Nonetheless, in order to justify the fact that the unbaptized, or the Negro or slave or female or whoever, did not have the same rights, one was compelled to claim that they were not fully human beings, as history cruelly witnesses.

(b) **No.** Because each culture expresses its experience of reality and of the humanum in concepts and symbols which are proper to that tradition and are as such not universal, and most likely not universalizable. This relationship between truth and the expression of truth in concepts and symbols is one of the most central philosophical problems. Truth has the inbuilt claim to be universally valid, here and there, yesterday and tomorrow, for you and for me. Yet my grasping and formulating it cannot sustain the same claim without charging all the others who do not agree with me with

> stupidity or wickedness. Hence the necessary *via media* between agnostic relativism and dogmatic absolutism. This is what can be called *relativity*.
>
> Our particular case is a typical example of the *pars pro toto*: from the optic of the inside it looks like the whole; from the outside it looks like a part, a fragment. Similarly, human rights are universal from the vantage point of modern Western culture, and not universal from the outside looking in. Now, if we take from the inside *pars pro toto*, are we able to take from the outside the *totum in parte*? Can another culture see in the human rights issue a universal language? Or should we say that it is only one way of looking at things, one way of speaking?

The answer which claims to discover the *totum in parte* is appealing, but not convincing. This is the temptation of the intellectual, who senses that any affirmation has the inbuilt tendency to be universally valid — or of the politician who, having neither the time nor the inclination to engage in such reflections, would like to see the *totum* in the *parte* of his party. But then we tend to become the self-appointed judges of all humankind. Now philosophy, being a situated reflection, makes us aware that nobody has direct access to the universal range of human experience. We can only indirectly and through a limited perspective come to know the totality. Even were we to know all the existing human opinions, ours would amount to just another opinion. One cannot view the *totum* except in and through one's own window. This is the case not only because the whole is more than the sum of its parts, but also because the *totum* does not exist independently from the *parte* through which it is seen. It is only seen in and through the respective *parte* and there is no stance from which one could proceed to the integration of all the parts. Co-existence is only possible on a common ground, a *co-esse* recognized by the different parties.

Here lies the crux. We cannot but aim at the *totum*, and yet we often forget that all we see is the *pars* which we then take *pro toto*. If a Christian, to put another example, were to say that Christ is not the universal saviour, according to accepted custom he or she would cease to be a Christian. But a non-Christian should not and cannot agree with this. It is only in mutual dialogue that their respective views will change or evolve. Christ will be for the Christian the symbol of totality; for the non-Christian, only the symbol of the Christians.

Myriad examples from the past, especially regarding the West, are all too striking for one not to be wary of the danger of repeating what was done in the name of the one God, the one Empire, the one Religion, and what is nowadays being done under the aegis of the one Science and the one Technology.

In brief, we need a new hermeneutic: the diatopical hermeneutic that can only be developed in a *dialogical* dialogue. This would show us that we must take neither the *pars pro toto*, nor believe that we see the *totum pro parte*, when we are aware of the *pars pro toto*; which is obviously what we will retort right back to him. This is the human condition and I would not consider it to be an imperfection. This, again, is the topic of the pluralism.

Let us consider now an example of a different perspective without attempting to present any homeomorphic equivalent.

An Indian Reflection

The word "Indian" here has no political connotations. It does not refer to the "nation" with the third largest Islamic population in the world, but to the traditional Hindu, Jain and Buddhist conceptions of reality.

Dharma (*dhamma*) is perhaps the most fundamental word on the Indian tradition which could lead us to the discovery of a possible homeomorphic symbol corresponding to the Western notion of "human rights". I am not advancing the idea that *dharma* is the homeomorphic equivalent of human rights. I am only indicating that a reflection at the level of *dharma* may help us find our footing on a common ground, so that we may know what we are looking for when we set out on our search for "human rights" in the classical Indian context.

As is well known, the meaning of the word *dharma* is multivocal: besides element, data, quality and origination, it means law, norm of conduct, character of things, right, truth, ritual, morality, justice, righteousness, religion, destiny, and many other things. It will not lead us anywhere to try to find an English common denominator for all these names, but perhaps etymology can show us the root metaphor underlying the many meanings of the word.[21] *Dharma* is that which maintains, gives cohesion and thus strength to any given thing, to reality, and ultimately to the three worlds (*triloka*). Justice keeps human relations together; morality keeps oneself in

---

21. A recent example: A Catholic missionary, after over a year of really living together with an Asian tribe and sharing with the people their respective beliefs, thinks that the moment has come for some formal conversions, since they are already practically Christians. He talks matters over with the enthusiasts about Christianity: "Would you like to become officially and publicly Christians? You are already convinced . . ." *etcetera*. Answer: "No, because some other people in the tribe are not ready." "But it is your *right*!," says the missionary, "you have the *right* to decide by yourselves — all the more since you neither harm nor despise the others." The answer is cutting: "We only have the right to take this step if the whole tribe does it."

harmony; law is the binding principle for human relations; religion is what maintains the universe in existence; destiny is that which links us with our future; truth is the internal cohesion of a thing; a quality is what pervades a thing with a homogeneous character; an element is the minimum consistent particle, spiritual or material; and the like.

Now a world in which the notion of *dharma* is central and nearly all-pervasive is not concerned with finding the "right" of one individual against another or of the individual *vis-à-vis* society, but rather with assaying the dhārmic (*right, true,* consistent . . .) or adhārmic character of a thing or an action within the entire theanthropocosmic complex of reality.

Dharma is primordial. We cannot hope to understand it if we approach it with moral categories (cf. the case of the *Gītā*) or even epistemological ones. It embraces both the conflict and the resolution; both the ought and the ought not. There is no universal *dharma* above and independent of the *svadharma*, the *dharma* which is inherent in every being. And this *svadharma* is at the same time a result of and a reaction to the *dharma* of everyone else.

The starting point here is not the individual, but the whole complex concatenation of the Real. In order to protect the world, for the sake of the protection of this universe, says Manu, He, *Svayambhu*, the self-existent, arranged the castes and their duties.[22] *Dharma* is the order of the entire reality, that which keeps the world together.[23] The individual's duty is to maintain his "rights"; it is to find one's place in relation to society, to the cosmos, and to the transcendent world.

22. From the root *dhr*, to hold, to maintain, keep together. Cf. Latin *tenere* and English *tenet*.

23. Manu, I, 31 and I, 87.

It is obvious from these brief paragraphs that here the discourse on "human rights" would take on an altogether different character. It would distract us from the purpose of this article to look now for the homeomorphic equivalent of human rights in a culture pervaded with the conception of *dharma*. We adduce this Indian example only to be able to elaborate in a fuller way the question of our title.

Only one submission and one observation may be allowed here so as not to leave this thought incomplete. I submit that the homeomorphic equivalent is *svadharma*, and I make the observation that the homeomorphic equivalent does not mean the corresponding counterpart, as if all that is conveyed by human rights is also borne by *svadharma* or vice versa. Cultures are wholes, and do not fit into one-to-one correspondences. In order to have a just society, the modern West stresses the notion of human rights. In order to have a dhārmic order, classical India stresses the notion of *svadharma*.

We shall now attempt to formulate without further development some reactions to the Western discourses on human rights from this Indian perspective. We should add immediately that this Indian critique does not imply that the Indian model is better, or that Indian culture has been faithful to its fundamental intuition — as the existence of the outcastes and the degeneration of the caste system sufficiently prove. In confrontation and dialogue with the Western model, the Indian critique would stress fundamentally that human rights should not be absolutized. It would contest that one can speak of human rights as "objective" entities standing on their own in isolation from the rest of the real. This is what seems to be implied in the very first article of the declaration: "All human beings are born free and equal in dignity and rights. They are endowed with reason and conscience and should act towards one another in a spirit of brotherhood." Particular rights, privileges due to a special position in society, i.e. a relativization of rights does not seem to be compatible with this article.

Developing this point, the Indian vision would insist on the following points among others:

1. Human rights are not individual human rights only. The *humanum* is not incarnated in the individual *only*. The individual as such is an abstraction, and an abstraction as such cannot be an ultimate subject of rights. As we have already indicated, the individual is only the knot in and of the net of relationships which form the fabric of the Real. The knots may individually be all the same (either *jīva, ātmā,* or *anātmā*), but it is mainly their position in the net which determines the set of "rights" an individual may have. Individuality is not a substantial category, but a functional one. The structure of the universe is hierarchical, but this does not imply that the higher echelons have the right to trample upon the rights of the lower ones — in spite of the dangers of this happening the moment the harmony of the whole is disturbed.

   I am not entering into the merits or demerits of this world view. We should however bear in mind that this conception is intimately linked with the conception of *karma,* and thus should not be evaluated outside its proper context.

2. Human rights are not human only. They concern equally the entire cosmic display of the universe, from which even the gods are not absent. The animals, all the sentient beings

and the supposedly inanimate creatures, are also involved in the interaction concerning "human" rights. Man is a peculiar being, to be sure, but neither alone nor so essentially distinct. One could even ask whether there are specific human rights, or if this specificity is again only an abstraction for pragmatic reasons which defeats its own purpose the moment we forget its merely practical character.

Here again, another cosmology and another theology provide the justification for this conception. Whether modern India, accepting and adopting modern science as it is, will be able to maintain this conception for very long is another matter altogether. But we know also about the persistence of mythical patterns.

3. Human rights are not rights only. They are also duties and both are interdependent. Humankind has the "right" to survive only in so far as it performs the duty of maintaining the world (*lokasamgraha*). We have the "right" to eat only inasmuch as we fulfil the duty of allowing ourselves to be eaten by a hierarchically higher agency. Our right is only a participation in the entire metabolic function of the universe.

   We should have, if anything, a declaration of Universal Rights and Duties in which the whole of Reality would be encompassed. Obviously, this demands not only a different anthropology but also a different cosmology and an altogether different theology — beginning with its name. That only human beings and not animals could make this declaration would invalidate it only to the same extent that the declaration of Human Rights could be contested because the Nagas and the Masai did not take part in the discussion and framing of the declaration.

4. Human rights are not mutually isolatable. They are related not only to the whole cosmos and all their corresponding duties; they form, among themselves as well, a harmonious whole. It is for this reason that a material list of definitive human rights is not theoretically feasible. It is the universal harmony that ultimately counts. This is not invalidated by the fact that India, as so many other countries, knows the codification of laws. India suffers, perhaps more than most countries, from legalistic *minutiae*, precisely because no judicial legislation will ever suffice.[24]

5. Human rights are not absolute. They are intrinsically relative, they are relationships among entities. Moreover, these entities are determined by the relationships themselves. To say that my human value depends on my position in the universe would be a caricature of what has been said if we start by thinking of an individual in itself,

---

24. Cf. the famous *lokasamgraha* of the *Gītā*, and the well-known definition of the *Mahābhārata*: "that which maintains and sustains the peoples." (Karṇaparvam, LXIX, 59).

A recent example may illuminate the issue: In July 1981, the Indian nation is in an uproar because some 352 outcastes of the small village of Minakshipuram in Tamil Nadu converted to Islam, probably in protest and reaction against their ostracism (to say the least) from the Hindu caste-communities. For our point it is interesting to remark that HH, Sri Vishveshva Tirtha Swamiji of Pejavar Muṭṭ along with many other Hindu religious leaders can now — for obviously political and opportunistic reasons — raise their voices against untouchability and discrimination without paying attention to the *Mānavadharmaśāstra* (III, 92, 150, 157; IV, 79, 213; IX, 238-39; etc.) and other sacred laws sanctioning the system. Cf. the Indian press from May to August, 1981; e.g. *The Hindu* from Madras, May 26; July 15-16, 18, 28-30; August 2; etc.

whose dignity is then made to depend on whether he or she is rich or poor, of one caste or another, etc. The classical Indian vision would not subscribe to this — in spite of the failures of the system in the praxis and even the degeneration in time — but it would start from a holistic conception and then define a portion of reality by function of its situation in the totality. In a certain sense, the knot is nothing — because it is the whole net.

6. Both systems (the Western and the Hindu) make sense from and within a given and accepted myth. Both systems imply a certain kind of consensus. When that consensus is challenged, a new myth must be found. The broken myth is the situation in India today, as it is in the world at large. That the rights of individuals be conditioned only by their position in the net of reality can no longer be admitted by the contemporary mentality. Nor does it seem to be admissible that the rights of individuals be so absolute as not to depend at all on the particular situation of the individual.

   In short, there is at present no endogenous theory capable of unifying contemporary societies and no imposed or imported ideology can be simply substituted for it. A mutual fecundation of cultures is a human imperative of our times.

   The declaration defends the individual from the abuses of the State or society. The Indian view would say that we are part of a harmonious whole on pilgrimage toward a non-historical goal. Interactions are the very warp and woof of the universe. Cultural and religious traditions offer a whole that cannot easily be dismembered without doing violence to their insights. Hindu *karma* outside its context may become fatalistic. Christian charity outside its system may turn oppressive. The universalization of human rights is a very delicate question indeed.

By Way of Conclusion

Is the concept of human rights a Western conception?

Yes.

Should the world then renounce declaring or enforcing human rights?

No.

Three qualifications, however, are necessary.

1. For an authentic human life to be possible within the *megamachine* of the modern technological world, human rights are imperative. This is because the development of the notion of human rights is bound up with and given its meaning by the slow development of that megamachine. How far individuals or groups or nations should collaborate with this present-day system is another question altogether. But in the contemporary political arena as defined by current socio-economic and ideological trends, the defence of human rights is a sacred duty. Yet it should be remembered that to introduce human rights (in the definite Western sense, of course) into other cultures before the introduction of *techniculture* would amount not only to putting the cart before the horse, but also to preparing the way for the technological invasion — as if by a Trojan horse, as we have already said. And yet a technological civilization without human rights amounts to the most inhuman situation imaginable. The dilemma is excruciating. This makes the two following points all the more important and urgent.

2. Room should be made for other traditions to develop and formulate their homeomorphic views corresponding to or opposing Western "rights". Or rather, these other world traditions should make room for themselves, since no one else is likely to make it for them. This is an urgent task; otherwise it will be impossible for non-Western cultures to survive, let alone to offer viable alternatives or even a sensible complement. Here the role of a cross-cultural philosophical approach is paramount. The need for human pluralism is often recognized in principle, but not often practised, not only because of the dynamism which drives the paneconomic ideology, linked with the megamachine, to expand all over the world, but also because viable alternatives are not yet theoretically worked out.
3. An intermediary space should be found for mutual criticism that strives for mutual fecundation and enrichment. Perhaps such an interchange may help bring forth a new myth and eventually a more humane civilization. The dialogical dialogue appears as the unavoidable method.

   Perhaps a suggestion here may prove helpful. Playing on the metaphor of the knots (individuality) and the net (personhood) we could probably affirm that traditional cultures have stressed the net (kinship, hierarchical structure of society, the function to be performed, the role of each part in relation to the whole), so that often the knot has been suffocated and not allowed sufficient free space for its own self-identity. On the other hand, modernity stresses the knot (individual free will to choose any option, the idiosyncrasies of everyone, the atomization of society) so that often the knot has been lost in loneliness, alienated by its own social mobility, and wounded (or killed) in competition with other more powerful knots. Perhaps the notion of personhood as the interplay between the knots and the net, as well as the realization that freedom is not just the capacity to choose between given options but also the power to create options, could provide a starting point for the proposed mutual fecundation.

If many traditional cultures are centred on God, and some other cultures basically cosmocentric, the culture which has come up with the notion of human rights is decisively anthropocentric. Perhaps we may now be prepared for a cosmotheandric vision of reality in which the divine, the human and the cosmic are integrated into a whole, more or less harmonious according to the performance of our truly human rights.[25]

---

25. This article appeared originally in *Diogenes*, Number 120 (Winter 1982) pp. 75-102. Reprinted with permission.

3

A Response

Arvind Sharma

I WAS delighted to receive your paper entitled: "Is the Notion of Human Rights a Western Concept?" which appeared in *Diogenes* (120: 75-102 [Winter 1982]). I had heard people mention it and then I saw a colleague cite it, but my interest in the issue of human rights was quickened only recently, as a result of my participation in the project on Religion and Human Rights at the instance and by the example of Professor Harvey Cox. However, even though your paper is more than a decade old I feel compelled to respond and raise certain issues for the clarification and enrichment of my own ideas, for your remarks remain as relevant today as when they were first made.

1. On page 32 (lines 10-14), you seem to voice philosophical objections to the concept of universality by raising the very pertinent point: "Does it make sense to ask about conditions of universality when the very question about conditions of universality is far from universal?" If we keep in mind that such an interrogative formulation *itself* might be approved by a number of scholars, who might well differ about these very conditions of universality, how would we feel if the word *consensual* were substituted for universal? In other words, if we bracketed your misgivings about human rights discourse in general momentarily, what would be your reaction to a *consensual* declaration of human rights? The point whether universality is itself universal could also be put on the philosophical shelf.

2. On page 34 (lines 2-3), you raise the question of the relationship of human rights to human dignity implicitly by conceding the assumption that a notion of human rights may be "absolutely necessary to guarantee human dignity." In the text of the Universal Declaration of Human Rights, especially in the opening statement of the preamble and in Article 1, human rights and human dignity are spoken of in the same breath and appear to have been treated symmetrically though not synonymously (semantically speaking). Am I right in assuming that you question this equation of the two by raising such (potential questions) as:

   (a) Are human rights absolutely indispensable to guarantee human dignity?

   (b) Do human rights constitute the basis of human dignity? or

   (c) Does human dignity constitute the basis of human rights?

   (d) Can human rights and human dignity come in conflict?

   In fact on page 34 (lines 20-21), one encounters the following comment: "If, for instance, human rights are the exercise of and respect of human dignity. . . ." To me the provisional "if" seems important. Harvey Cox has argued, for instance, that Blacks in America have often displayed human dignity without possessing human rights. Would you agree?

3. The idea of homeomorphic equivalence is developed on pages 34 and 35. In this respect I would like to raise the following issues:

   (a) From the point of view of the phenomenology of religion, I find it instructive that you opt for homeomorphic and not *homomorphic* equivalence, as in the case of both "primitive" humans and "modern" humans *both* possessing a primitive or magical and modern or scientific mentality, not as stages in the evolution of human consciousness but as two distinct states of human consciousness. I am therefore tempted to ask, whether you consider the phenomenological approach more congenial to current human rights discourse than a hermeneutical approach?;

(b) If one follows through on footnote 4 on page 34, then with Aquinas' views on the analogical nature of language in mind, could one propose that intra-traditional understanding may be analogical but a cross-cultural understanding is best approached homeomorphically?;

(c) If this be so then the homeomorphic equivalent of date rape in the West (when the partners negotiate their own marriage on the basis of physical attraction) would be equivalent of the institution of the dowry in India (when the parents negotiate the marriage on the basis of financial considerations). Note that homeomorphic *equivalence* has equated things apparently as far apart as violence and greed. Of course one might well pause to wonder whether they are in fact that far apart;

(d) Functional equivalence involves comparability of functions; but what if one culture functions in such a way as to be devoid of the function being considered?;

(e) Is it not possible and even likely that the homeomorphic equivalence of what is *legal* in nature in one culture may turn out to be what is *moral* in another. In fact could it not happen to the human rights system as a whole, it being treated as constituting legality in one culture but morality in another?

4. On page 35 (lines 15-17), you employ the useful simile of the windows. In fact I feel like citing the passage to savour it again.

   In order to clarify the question of our title, I shall indicate some of the assumptions on which the notion of human rights is based and immediately insert some cross-cultural reflections which will lead us to the *locus* — the context — of the question and the justification for my answer, which I would like to anticipate by means of a simile: Human rights are one window through which one particular culture envisages a just human order for its individuals. But those who live in that culture do not see the window. For this they need the help of another culture which sees through another window. Now I assume that the human landscape as seen through the one window is both similar to and different from the vision of the other. If this is the case, should we smash the windows and make of the many portals a single gaping aperture — with the consequent danger of structural collapse — or should we enlarge the viewpoints as much as possible and, most of all, make people aware that there are — and have to be — a plurality of windows? This latter option would be the one in favour of a healthy pluralism.

   But what if religions and cultures are like *stained glass* windows instead of see-through windows?

5. On page 36 (footnote 5), you state: "I shall capitalize human rights when these words have the particular meaning derived from the Universal Declaration of Human Rights." This suggests to me a very useful distinction between

human rights in the lower case as an ethical concept and in the higher case as a legal concept. How would you react to that? Even the further concept of *humane* rights, such as those of *handicapped* human beings could also be placed alongside the other two.

Or would you prefer human rights in the lower case as an ontological category instead of a moral one? I am tempted to make this point on account of your familiarity with Hindu thought. If human rights are ethical in nature, then they approximate the position of Pūrvamīmāṁsā, wherein the injunctions are knowable only through the Vedas by definition. Śaṅkara writes in his commentary on *Brahmasūtra* I.1.3 that *brahman* is different from *dharma* because it is ontological (*bhūtaviṣaya*) in nature and therefore, unlike *dharma*, an existent which is given and not a rule or injunction to be obeyed. If we replace the Vedas by the Constitution as the source of authority then the striking significance of this distinction becomes clear. If human rights are legal or even moral, they can change with changing legal codes and moral views because they are *generators* of it. They can even be taken away. If, however, they are ontological in nature then any system of human rights can only be an expression of it and they can still be denied but they can never be deleted.

6. On page 39 (lines 13-15), you distinguish the individual *vis-à-vis* society and *vis-à-vis* the State. One could argue that, on account of the caste system, the Indian reality requires, in the case of India, that same attention be given to the *rightful* regulation of the relationship of the individual in relation to the society as is given to him or her in relation to the State in the West. What do you think of this

suggestion? And will this consideration not affect the way we perceive the issue of reservations for Scheduled Castes and Tribes and Other Backward Classes in India?

[The stakes are high and connect forward with point number (22) later]. The point at issue could be the very concept of equality. The early liberal version which prevailed in the U.S.A. and India was one of (a) equality of opportunity and treatment and one in which (b) the notion of the State relating directly to the citizen, and not a group, was dominant. This statist view is now being contested, particularly in India and partly in the U.S.A., by a societal one, in which (a) equality of results replaces equality of opportunity, with the allied notion that if necessary, difference in treatment (affirmative action) may be resorted to achieve equality of results and (b) the right to equality inheres not in a common nationality but rather flows from those possessed by a dispossessed group overagainst other groups which constitute the nation. The concept of "equal rights" in the Universal Declaration of Human Rights seems to me to be the statist one. Although group rights are apparently acknowledged in the documents which now comprise the International Bill of Human Rights I wonder if the allied shift involved in the concept of equality has been noticed.

7. On page 40 under item (c), you state that the assumption of the dignity of the individual inherent in the notion of human rights implies "resonances of the idea of *Man* as *microcosmos* and reverberations of the conviction that Man is *imago dei*, and at the same time the relative independence of this conviction from ontological and theological foundations." Scholars of religion tend to identify *imago*

dei as a theological resource for human rights, as affirming the "absolute and inestimable worth of the person."[1] However, one legal application of this principle is worth noting. The legal application (Genesis 9) of theological principle (Genesis 1) meant that no "economic exchange" was possible in the case of killing a human being, namely, murder. This raises at least two interesting points:

(a) Are the human rights a moral or a legal affirmation? The point to note is that the distance between the moral proclamation and its legal application is often full of surprises, which are sometimes not merely unpleasant but virtually negate the moral purpose; and

(b) the relative independence from theological formulations may sometimes be a good thing. Modern law, for instance, does not require that murder be avenged by murder; neither, I presume, did later Rabbinic Law?

8. Is there a danger of secular moral solipsism in maintaining that the "individual has an inalienable dignity because he is an end in himself and a kind of absolute"? (page 40, lines 18-19). I realize that you are here representing rather than presenting a view, but the issue might still be worth factoring into the human rights equation, for this solipsism is also at least partially blind. Although on the one hand it maintains that murder must match murder, on the other, to answer your question: "Can you kill one person to save another?" — the answer provided in Judaism is yes, for

1. See Michael Fishbane, "The Image of the Human and the Rights of the Individual in Jewish Tradition", in Leroy S. Rouner, ed., *Human Rights and the World's Religions*, Notre Dame, Indiana: University of Notre Dame Press, 1988, p. 18.

not only is that how the Jews justified the crucifixion of Jesus in relation to them, that is how Jesus justified it in relation to the rest of humanity! Perhaps a distinction has to be drawn here between (a) killing (i.e. murdering) someone else; (b) allowing oneself to be killed instead of having to oneself kill someone else; (c) allowing oneself to let someone else get killed in order to save the larger group and (d) allowing oneself to get killed to save humanity. Case (a) is forbidden by the first commandment; case (b) is represented by the following example:

> In every other law of the Torah, if a man is commanded, "Transgress and do not suffer death," he may transgress and not suffer death, excepting idolatry, incest, and shedding blood . . .. Murder may not be practised to save one's life . . .. Even as one who came before Raba and said to him: "The government of my town has ordered me, 'Go and kill so and so; if not I will slay you.'" Raba answered him: "Let him rather slay you than you should commit murder; *who knows that your blood is redder? Perhaps his blood is redder*!" (b. Sanhedrin 74a).[2]

Case (c) is represented by the example of Kaiaphas who says regarding Jesus' impending condemnation that it is better that one perish rather than many (John 18:13-14) and case (d) is represented by Jesus' vicarious atonement for the sin of humanity.

9. The question you ask in lines 20-21 of page 40 is: "You can cut off a finger for the sake of the entire body, but can you kill one person to save another?" Here the *theological* answer is of course no, as you (page 40, note 11) and others have pointed out, but in the light of what has just been said, does not the question now become a real one instead

2. Ibid., p. 20.

of being merely rhetorical? Article 5 forbids torture but given the reality of terrorism, what if the lives of hundreds hang on the thread by which the tortured terrorist's life hangs to obtain his or her crucial confession?

Would the human rights answer be yes in accordance with section 2 of Article 29? Be that as it may, my question is: Do you see individualism ultimately lapsing into some as yet undetermined kind of solipsism? I am led to ask this by the tendency in metaphysics, as well as morals, of that to which we accord *supreme* worth becoming the *sole* object of worth.

10. In footnote 12 on page 41, you cite clause 3 of Article 21: "The will of the people shall be the basis of the authority of the government." Does this not require that voting be compulsory? And is this will more appropriately expressed through a presidential than a prime ministerial form of democracy?

11. In footnote 13 on page 42 you cite clause 2 of Article 29, with the problematic words placed in italics. The Article deals with the limitation of an individual's rights by other individuals, especially those "meeting the *just* requirements of *morality, public order,* and the general welfare in a *democratic* society." Don't you think that considerations of *health* also be specifically included?

12. In lines 16-18 on page 42, you indicate that the declaration was "along the lines of historical trends of the Western world during the last three centuries . . ." Some scholars now maintain that while this might be true of the Universal Declaration of Human Rights in 1948, the subsequent documents, which comprise the International Bill of Human Rights mentioned in footnote 6 on page 36 of your

article, take the concerns of the non-Western world into account and should not be dubbed "Western". An article by Virginia A. Leary, "The Effect of Western Perspectives on International Human Rights", in Abdullah A. An-Maim and F. Deng (eds.), *Human Rights in Africa* (Washington, D.C.: Brookings Institution, 1990) pp. 15-30 is often cited in this regard. Would you then stand by in 1994 what you stated in 1982, or would you be inclined to revise your opinion in view of the developments which have occurred since you wrote your path-breaking piece?

13. On page 43 (lines 5-7) it is stated that "to accept the possibility of universal concepts would imply a strictly rationalistic conception of reality." Must this be the case? Emotional experience of love, hate, etc. would probably be accepted as universal. They admittedly belong to the realm of emotion, not reason; but, are they not capable of being "rationalized", thereby yielding a universal concept which is not strictly a rationalistic conception? (This criticism would, of course, not apply, if feeling and willing, along with thinking are subsumed in rationality). Moreover, what about the biological bases of such a universalism, inasmuch as hunger, thirst, etc. are our common lot. And what of the collective unconsciousness of Jung. Could human rights qualify as an archetype?

14. On page 43, lines 10-12, it is suggested that "to accept the fact that the concept of human rights *is* not universal does not yet mean that it *should* not *become* so." To be sure, something not yet universal may be universalized. The whole idea of cultural diffusion, not to mention the spread of technology from the Stone Age to our own times, confirms this. Did the idea of "eternity", which one takes so much for granted as to consider natural, originate in

Egypt? The same is true of language. We may not have a neutral universal language in the foreseeable future but English could well become universalized. My question pertains to whether the universalized really becomes universal. The ethnic explosions which follow the break-up of an apparently homogenized state may be a wake-up call in this respect. If human rights are universalized they may not only be viewed but remain as symbols of external power rather than nature; the imposition by a few beings on others of certain norms in the name of humanity. One may have to guard against this.

A second question arises in the same context, regarding the lines which follow the one cited above: "Now in order for a concept to become universally valid it should fulfil at least two conditions. It should, on the one hand, eliminate all the other contradictory concepts. This may seem improbable, but there is a logical necessity here and, theoretically, it would all be for the best. On the other hand, it should be the universal point of reference for any problems regarding human dignity. In other words, it should displace all other homeomorphic equivalents and be the pivotal centre of a just social order. To put it in another way, the culture which has given birth to the concept of human rights should also be called upon to become a universal culture. This may well be one of the causes of a certain uneasiness one senses in non-Western thinkers who study the question of human rights. They fear for the identity of their cultures" (page 43).

I think it might be possible to distinguish between the culture and the cultural product. Human rights could be the universal idea of a particular culture, just as the abolition of slavery might have been the universal idea of some particular culture. When it got universalized it genuinely became universal.

15. The whole discussion of Cross-Cultural Reflections (a) on pages 42-43, seems to be based on the equation of *uniformity* with universality. Are we missing an intermediate category of *uniformality*? Just as uniformity is not to be mistaken for universality, neither should *uniformality* be confused with *uniformity*. There need not be the same kinds of courts in relation to human rights in every country (uniformality) but the same ideals could be expressed in terms of local culture (universality). There could also be uniformity in this respect among some cultures.

16. I think you have hit upon a very important point in recognizing that there could be cases of doubt or conflict in relation to human rights, although the remark seems to have been made in passing (page 44, lines 16-17). I have long felt the need to recognize this dimension of human rights: that they may come in conflict. The problem does not end with recognition; it also requires resolution. Perhaps courts could help. Or perhaps not. Many of the human rights presuppose an ordered society, others a just society. Claims to justice, however, typically disturb the existing order. The point may be driven home by raising this question: Would you live in an *ordered* society or in a *just* society when a tradeoff is involved. The savant Will Durant remarks that as he matured his preference shifted towards order.

    This issue of priority among rights works at two levels. At one level there is the question of group rights, socio-economic rights, etc. versus individual rights, in terms of prioritization. Then there is the further issue of conflict within the rights at their own level. For instance, should the right to health take priority over education at the group level? How may their claims be adjusted? At the level of individual rights there is, for instance, the possibility of a conflict arising between the "right to freedom of opinion and expression" (Article 19) and what might be construed by the person in relation to whom this right is being exercised as an invasion of their privacy and an attack on their honour and reputation (Article 12).

In fact such conflicts can arise at an even more fundamental level, as between that of justice and the human rights themselves. Both are mentioned in the preamble. "As Taitetsu Unno asks poignantly in reflecting on Buddhist sensibilities "when *rights* are seen from a purely anthropocentric or egocentric perspective", as they are typically in dominant Western perspectives, "can we ever do *justice* to other forms of existence, animate and inanimate"?"[3]

17. On the face of it, it does seem to be the case that in the Declaration of Human Rights "there is no mention of the economic conditions for the effective realization of what are said to be universal claims" (page 45, lines 5-8). Two points may be worth noting in this respect, one more important than the other. The emergence of human rights themselves is connected by many scholars with the growth of capitalism. The right to property is considered particularly significant in this regard. So they do possess an implicitly economic dimension. There is also at least one explicit mention of this dimension in Article 23, although a similar point in section (2) of Article 27 seems

---

3. Taitetsu Unno, "Personal Rights and Contemporary Buddhism", in Leroy S. Rouner, ed., op. cit., p. 144.

to be aimed at protecting the economic interests of a specific group. There is, on the one hand, a general capitalist silence and a few specific capitalist claims on the other (Article 27 [2]). The influence of socialism has been traced in the subsequent documents but the two remain unreconciled. Even sections (1) and (2) of Article 27 seem to be in conflict. Observers have pointed out that the exercise of patent rights on medicine is seriously affecting their availability in Third World countries.

18. I think the point and the problem itself may not be the same is very well taken (page 46, lines 20-21). However, there could be similar problems and even the same problem in a different garb. There is also an allied insight, that "Rights are a way that we organize our conflicts. They are not a solution to conflicts, and do not offer final ends." Let me address these in succession.

    The question of freedom of religion does not appear in Hindu culture in the same way as in the Western, but it does surface as the doctrine of *adhikāra-bheda*. Its explanation could not differ more than that of Article 18 and yet the substance is the same:

    The doctrine of *adhikāri-bheda* is an application of this epistemological notion of absolute relatively to the specifically religious sphere. The difference of *adhikārī* or spiritual status is not necessarily a "gradation"; and so far as it is a gradation it does not suggest any relation of higher and lower that implies contempt or envy. The notion of *adhikāra* in fact means in the first instance just an acceptance of fact or realism in the spiritual sphere. It is a question of duty rather than of rights in this sphere; and a person should be anxious to discover his actual status in order that he may set before himself just such duties as he can efficiently perform in spirit. It is a far greater misfortune here to over-estimate one's status than to under-estimate it. A higher status does not mean greater opportunity for spiritual work, since work here means not outward achievement, but an inwardizing or deepening of the spirit. Again, from the standpoint of toleration, one not only respects the inner achievement of a person admitting an inferior status, but can whole-heartedly identify oneself with it; the highest *adhikārin* should feel it a privilege to join in the worship of the humblest. There is aristocracy in the spiritual polity; spiritual value is achieved by the strong and is much too sacred a thing to be pooled. At the same time every individual has his sacred *svadharma* and has equal opportunity with everyone else to realize or "inwardize" it.[4]

Yet although the *substance* is the same the *content* differs and the thrust of the Hindu version consists in allowing everyone the freedom to *follow* their own conscience or religion, while that of the Declaration of Human Rights consists in allowing everyone the freedom to change it. Now the allied insight could come into play. *Duty* idiom may be more consistent with following the same course; *rights* idiom with changing it. Thus the manner in which we organize our conflicts has a bearing on how we resolve them.

---

4. Krishnachandra Bhattacharyya, "The Advaita and Its Spiritual Significance", in Haridas Bhattacharyya, ed., *The Cultural Heritage of India,* Calcutta: The Ramakrishna Mission Institute of Culture, 1955, vol. III, p. 252.

19. I am glad you feel that cross-cultural access is possible (page 50, paragraph 1), for often people take an extreme view that this is just not possible. I am also glad you did not take the line that what if human rights represent moral imperialism, for any point of view which claims to take into account all other views is essentially imperialistic, and in this sense one cannot escape imperialism in any form of universalism. Dual cultural citizenship is possible, however.

20. I strongly agree with your point that the very articulation of human rights, although it might not be a sign of desperation may yet hint at the fact of their erosion (page 49, lines 7-16). At the same time silence about human rights does not mean their absence, no more than their formulation amounts to their implementation.

21. I think the distinction you draw between validity and universal validity or universality in the lines 5-10 of page 43 is extremely important. For one thing, it draws attention to the point, patent in comparative religion, between ethnic and universal religions. There is a dimension of universalism even in ethnic religions and a parochialism even in the universalism of so-called world religions. Next, just as ethnic religions can contain a universal dimension, there may be a universal assertion of ethnic rights and even an ethnic assertion of universal rights. Philosophically your statement is very significant because something may be wholly true and yet not true on the whole.

22. The idea that human rights might act as a kind of a cultural Trojan horse (page 50, lines 24-26), I think, needs to be taken with the utmost seriousness. And even more so your point that people "might be obliged to accept those ways of living, thinking and feeling for which human rights is

the proper solution in cases of conflict." It has even been argued by Professor Jacob Neusner that Judaism in fact first creates the problem for which it then offers a solution.[5] One might wish to argue this of religions in general. Thus Christianity first creates the very sense of sin from which Jesus offers salvation. Buddhism first heightens the sense of suffering and then offers Nirvāṇa.

However, in the field of cultural impact it does often happen that the dominant culture first creates the very problem for which it offers a solution. It is the West, for instance, which first deprived India of the right to self-determination and is then conferred by Article 21 of the Universal Declaration of Human Rights, about which it is "an undeniable fact that Western cultural influences shaped"[6] it. To one who hails from the East this fits into a disturbingly familiar pattern. India is first impoverished by foreign rule[7] and then economic aid is extended to it and so on.

23. It is difficult to disagree with your statement (page 51, lines 13-14) that "Rights cannot be abstracted from duties; the two are correlated." This sounds well in theory but may not be reflected in practice. People can be denied their rights in real life, they can be exploited, and in that sense, in practice, rights can be abstracted from duties.

    Hindu thought places a lot of emphasis on this correlation and even gives priority to duties. Mahatma Gandhi's

---

5. Jacob Neusner, "Judaism", in Arvind Sharma, ed., *Our Religions,* San Francisco: Harper, 1993, pp. 334 ff.
6. John Kelsey and Suner B. Twiss, eds., op. cit., p. 31.
7. R.C. Majumdar, *British Paramountcy and Indian Renaissance,* Bombay: Bharatiya Vidya Bhavan, 1991, vol. II, pp. 421 ff.

position on this point is well known. This aspect of it has also impressed many in the West. Thus Louis Renou says:

> But ambivalence is characteristic of India: for her, what is the good of killing her cows if she has to lose her soul? A factor in social and psychical equilibrium is found in the notion of *dharma* with its rigorous justice and the "truth" which it implies (the Indians insist on the attitude of truthfulness as others insist on an "attitude of consciousness.") An important consequence of this is tolerance, non-violence considered an active virtue; this is a manner of acting which must be respected — even in the political sphere — *regardless of the attitude of others*. In this perhaps is to be found the most spectacular contribution which India has made to the modern world and the most worthy reply to Marxism and its materialism.[8]

However, deontological exploitation is a real possibility and "rights" language may be necessary to assert them if they have been obscured. The crucial point to consider here is whether in order to perform one's duty, one only needs to know what is *right* rather than what are one's rights.

24. Your remarks on the deprivation of human rights in a way which affects an individual, yet cannot be directly attached to him, is remarkably perceptive. Under colonialism, it was this kind of deprivation which was felt even more keenly by the oppressed cultures with a sense of communal rather than individual identity. Thus, as you say, "The dignity of the human person may equally be violated by

---

8. Louis Renou, ed., *Hinduism*, New York: Braziller, 1962, pp. 55-56.

your language, or by your desecrating a place I consider holy, even though it does not belong to me in the sense of individual private property" (page 51). Lord Lytton going through the Golden Temple at Amritsar, without taking off his shoes, is a good example of such bad behaviour.[9]

25. The corporate nature of human rights, which you speak of on pages 50-52, demands more recognition, if only as a check against the abuse of the individual version of human rights, which results in reckless individualism and a proneness to litigation such as destroys the moral character of human rights by emphasizing their legal character. Both these points emerge into clear focus in the following comments on human rights made by Frederick Bird: He refers to two ambiguities in the notion of human rights and points out that

> it is impossible to think of rights as being the properties of isolated individuals. Particular rights exist as moral realities only where they are publicly recognized and enforced by institutional means. In practice, the honouring of these rights, then, is tied to political and legal activities of particular communities. Hence, human rights only gain practical recognition as prerogatives of individuals as members of particular political jurisdictions. *They might thus best be described not as human rights but as citizenship*

---

9. Satyendranath Tagore and Indira Devi, trs., *The Autobiography of Maharshi Devendranath Tagore,* London: Macmillan & Co., 1914 p. 216.: "Christians and Mohamadens, all may come here; only according to the rules none may enter the bounds of the Gurudwara with shoes on. All the Sikhs felt deeply humiliated and aggrieved by this rule being transgressed by the Governor-General, Lord Lytton."

> *rights.* This universal might then be rephrased in these words: all human communities ought to recognize that their members possess certain fundamental rights to non-interference from others, to exercise their own powers, and to fair distribution of benefits designated as communal goods. Stated in these terms the notion of human rights is necessarily connected with assumptions regarding human communities as responsible for and to the individuals who produce and re-produce them by their consents and actions.[10]

He goes on to identify the second ambiguity as follows:

> When groups of individuals too ardently pursue their rights as members of particular communities, there may be occasions or situations in which communal good will become exhausted. Quite independently of the legitimacy of any particular claim, communities are able to recognize and honour new rights only to the degree that historical pre-conditions allow. It is easier to honour rights that protect against abusive interference by others and rights that recognize the power of individuals to enter into contracts, to vote, and to hold property, than it is to honour those rights which call for the fair distribution of communal goods. Whether these goods are defined as tax dollars to be used for education, health services, or day care programmes, or as empty lands of settlement, or natural resources to be utilized, they are limited. These limits are set by the resources and goodwill of the community. As a result, the claims to honour particular rights, such as tax benefits for homeowners, may conflict with claims with

---

10. Frederick Bird, "Moral Universals", *The Journal of Religious Pluralism,* III: 74, 1993.

respect to other rights such as the right to decent health care services. *As these claims and counter claims mount, the notion of human rights becomes increasingly politicized. It loses its status as a moral universal and becomes merely a contentious assertion of particular wants and desires.*[11]

26. The remarks apropos the uniqueness of human rights I found exhilarating, especially in the following lines 18-24 (page 54): "The Declaration of Human Rights needs to be considered, at least in its intention, as a declaration with universal validity. To say that human rights are not universal would amount to saying that they are not human; they would cease to be *human* rights. The whole novelty of the declaration lies precisely here, in the assertion that every human being, by the mere fact of being human, is endowed with inalienable rights that everybody should respect."

    But then a painful reflection overtook me. Human rights have been contested — by human beings. Human rights have also been compromised — by human beings. So the claim to universality is really a potential, not a fully realized claim. Would it make more sense to speak of *common* rights which all accept not by virtue of our being human but by virtue of our having consciously accepted them. Some of the mystique is lost no doubt but perhaps enforceability is enhanced. The para preceding Article 1 in the Universal Declaration of Human Rights seems to anticipate this point implicitly but perhaps it requires explication.

27. The whole of the last para on page 54 ending on next page 55, strongly evokes the Hindu term *adhikāra*. The word is often used to translate the English word *rights* in Indian

11. Ibid., pp. 74-75.

languages in modern usage, but it acquires a very different resonance once the traditional expression *adhikārabhdeda* is invoked and the discourse flips back into rights and duties.

28. The last few lines of the second para on page 55 give the bad news: "Nonetheless, in order to justify the fact that the unbaptized, or the Negro or slave or female or whoever, did not have the same rights, one was compelled to claim that they were not fully human beings, as history cruelly witnesses."

    The good news is that human rights must be so natural a concept in some way that people could not be deprived of them without *dehumanizing* them first!

29. It is true that "Even were we to know all the existing human opinions, ours would amount to just another opinion" (page 56). However, if we know all existing opinions then the remark is quantitatively true but not qualitatively. Could one even say, *pace* Marx, that a change in quantity has led to change in quality?

30. If for Christians, Christ is the symbol of totality and for non-Christians only a symbol of the Christians (page 57, lines 9-11), could not the same be said of human rights, that they are a symbol of the totality of humanity for the West, but only a symbol of the West for non-Westerners?

* * *

Perhaps I should stop here. The Universal Declaration of Human Rights contains thirty articles and I have responded to your reflection on its Western connection with thirty points as well. Symmetry demands that I stop at this point.

I do not know whether you consider this letter worthy of a response, but as grace bears no relation to its being merited or unmerited (as I [mis]understand Christianity) perhaps I should not despair of receiving one. I need hardly add how honoured I would feel if you chose to share your response.

Conclusion

THIS book is about human rights as a Western concept. That description challenges their universality. The first chapter was therefore devoted to the various understandings the concept of universality, and allied concepts, could generate in either a contrastive or a complementary way. This provided the backdrop for Professor Panikkar's interrogation: Is the Notion of Human Rights a Western Concept?

Although this piece was published in 1982, its relevance has grown rather than diminished with the passage of time. The issues it raised remain as germane to human rights discourse today as they were when first articulated. It therefore provoked a ready response from Arvind Sharma when he read it in the early 1990s.

The issues raised therein are still before us. If anything, the events of 11 September, 2001 have thrown them into sharper relief. Perhaps in this concluding chapter one might put the issue of the universality of human rights in its broadest context: as part of the larger issue of the relationship of the West to the rest of the world. The core issue here is the universal relevance of Western culture, since it is this culture which claims to be the standard-bearer of human rights. The remarks of Samuel P. Huntington on the question of the universal relevance of Western culture deserve serious consideration at this point. He writes:

> Cultural and civilizational diversity challenges the Western and particularly American belief in the universal relevance of Western culture. This belief is expressed both descriptively and normatively. Descriptively it holds that peoples in all societies want to adopt Western values, institutions, and practices. If they seem not to have that desire and to be committed to their own traditional cultures, they are victims of a "false consciousness" comparable to that which Marxists found among proletarians who supported capitalism. Normatively the Western universalist belief posits that people throughout the world should embrace Western values, institutions, and culture because they embody the highest, most enlightened, most liberal, most rational, most modern, and most civilized thinking of humankind.[1]

According to Samuel Huntington such a view "suffers from three problems: it is false; it is immoral; and it is dangerous."[2] It is false because, as the events of 11 September, 2001 clearly demonstrate, it can no longer be assumed that the superiority of Western culture is that self-evident to the rest of the world. It is immoral, according to him, because "imperialism is the necessary logical consequence of (such) universalism."[3] And it is dangerous, as demonstrated once again by the events of 11 September, 2001. What then should the West's position be? Samuel Huntington is quite forthright in his analysis in this respect and deserves to be cited in full.

> All civilizations go through similar processes of emergence, rise and decline. The West differs from other civilizations

---

1. Samuel P. Huntington, *The Clash of Civilizations and the Remaking of the World Order*, New York: Simon & Schuster, 1996, p. 310.
2. Ibid.
3. Ibid.

> not in the way it has developed but in the distinctive character of its values and institutions. These include most notably its Christianity, pluralism, individualism, and rule of law, which made it possible for the West to invent modernity, expand throughout the world, and become the envy of other societies. In their ensemble these characteristics are peculiar to the West. Europe, as Arthur M. Schlesinger, Jr., has said, is "the source — the *unique* source" of the "ideas of individual liberty, political democracy, the rule of law, human rights, and cultural freedom. . . . These are *European* ideas, not Asian, nor African, nor Middle Eastern ideas, except by adoption." They make Western civilization unique, and Western civilization is valuable not because it is universal but because it *is* unique. The principal responsibility of Western leaders, consequently, is not to attempt to reshape other civilizations in the image of the West, which is beyond their declining power, but to preserve, protect, and renew the unique qualities of Western civilization. Because it is the most powerful Western country, that responsibility falls overwhelmingly on the United States of America.[4]

To stop here however would be to stop short. The dialogue which constitutes the core of this book serves to demonstrate that societies may be unique but that does not mean that they are thereby prevented from being universal, for each can be universal in its own unique way. The way to move forward in human rights discourse is to let different cultures and civilizations articulate the moral intuitions which lie at the heart of the human rights discourse in their own unique way.

---

4. Ibid., p. 311.

Bibliography

Baxi, Upendra, 2002, *The Future of Human Rights*, New Delhi: Oxford University Press.

Benn, S.I. (ed.), 1967, *The Encyclopedia of Philosophy*, New York: Macmillan.

Bhattacharyya, Krishnachandra, "The Advaita and Its Spiritual Significance", in Haridas Bhattacharyya (ed.), *The Cultural Heritage of India*, vol. III, Kolkata: The Ramakrishna Mission Institute of Culture.

Bird, Frederick, "Moral Universals", *The Journal of Religious Pluralism*, III (1993) pp. 29-83.

Fishbane, Michael, 1988, "The Image of the Human and the Rights of the Individual in the Jewish Tradition", in S. Leroy Rouner (ed.), *Human Rights and the World's Religions*, Notre Dame, Indiana: University of Notre Dame.

Glendon, Mary Ann, 2001, *The World Made New: Eleanor Roosevelt and the Universal Declaration of Human Rights*, New York: Random House.

Guardian Weekly, Feb. 2-8, 2007.

Huntington, Samuel P., 1996, *The Clash of Civilizations and the Remaking of the World Order*, New York: Simon & Schuster.

Kelsay, John and Sumner B. Twiss, 1994, *Religion and Human Rights*, New York: The Project for Religion and Human Rights.

King, Winsten L., 2005, "Religion: First Edition", in Lindsay Jones, editor in chief, *Encyclopedia of Religion* (second edition) vol. 11, Farmington Hills, MI: Thomson & Gale.

Lewis, Bernard, 1993, *Islam and the West*, New York: Oxford University Press.

Majumdar, R.C., 1991, ed., *British Paramountcy and Indian Renaissance*, vol. II, Mumbai: Bharatiya Vidya Bhavan.

Mozumdar, Suman Guha, 2006, "Kishore Mahbubani", *India Abroad*, Dec. 8, 2006, p. 14.

Neusner, Jacob, 1993, "Judaism", in Arvind Sharma, ed., *Our Religions*, San Francisco: Harper.

Oxtoby, Willard G., 1983, *The Meaning of Other Faiths*, Philadelphia: The Westminster Press.

Panikkar, R., 1982, "Is the Notion of Human Rights a Western Concept", *Diogenes*, (Winter 1982) Number 120, pp. 75-102.

——— 1980, "Aporias in the Comparative Philosophy of Religion", *Man in World*, XIII, 3-4 (1980) pp. 357-83.

——— 1979, *Myth, Faith and Hermeneutics*, New York: Paulist Press.

——— 1978, *The Intrareligious Dialogue*, New York: Paulist Press.

——— 1975, "Singularity and Individuality: The Double Principle of Individuation", *Revue internationale de philosophie*, XIX, 1-2, no. 111-12, pp. 141-66.

Renou, Louis, 1962, *Hinduism*, New York: Braziller.

Sidorsky, D., ed., 1979, *Essays on Human Contemporary Issues and Jewish Perspectives*, Philadelphia: The Jewish Publication Society of America.

Stackhouse, Max L., 2005, "Missions: Missionary Activity", in Lindsay Jones, editor in chief, *Encyclopedia of Religion* (second edition) vol. 9, Farmington Hills, MI: Thomson & Gale.

Tagore, Satyendranath and Indira Devi (eds.), *The Autobiography of Maharshi Devendranath Tagore*, London: Macmillan & Co.

Talking India: Ashis Nandy in Conversation with Ramin Jahanbegloo, 2006, New Delhi: Oxford University Press.

Unno, Taitetsu, "Personal Rights and Contemporary Buddhism", in S. Leroy Rouner, ed., *Human Rights and the World's Religions*, Notre Dame, Indiana: University of Notre Dame.

Weiss, Ruth R., 1992, *If I Am Not For Myself: The Liberal Betrayal of the Jews*, New York: The Free Press.

Index